SAINTS AND
SCHOLARS

SAINTS AND SCHOLARS

Twenty-five medieval portraits

BY

DAVID KNOWLES

*Regius Professor of Modern History in the
University of Cambridge and
Fellow of Peterhouse*

CAMBRIDGE
AT THE UNIVERSITY PRESS
1962

PUBLISHED BY

THE SYNDICS OF THE CAMBRIDGE UNIVERSITY PRESS

Bentley House, 200 Euston Road, London, N.W. 1
American Branch: 32 East 57th Street, New York 22, N.Y.
West African Office: P.O. Box 33, Ibadan, Nigeria

©

CAMBRIDGE UNIVERSITY PRESS

1962

Printed in Great Britain at the University Press, Cambridge
(Brooke Crutchley, University Printer)

FOREWORD

THIS book owes its existence to a suggestion made some years ago by Mr Oscar Watson, then of the Cambridge University Press. It is a collection of short biographies or character sketches taken, with two exceptions, from *The Monastic Order in England* and the three volumes of *The Religious Orders in England*. The exceptions are the pieces on Bede the Venerable and Anselm of Canterbury, which were written for broadcasting, but never published. The collection has been made in the hope that some readers who do not possess, and who would never have occasion to read, the larger volumes, might be interested in a series of portraits of medieval monks and others, some of them celebrated, others almost unknown. As these miniature biographies are taken almost as they stand from a larger context, they must not be considered as full-sized accounts or assessments of the men concerned, nor does the length of the chapter bear any relation to the importance of its subject. St Anselm, for example, is on every count a more significant figure than William More or Uthred of Boldon, but it so happened that I had no occasion to treat him at any length.

The passages are essentially unchanged from their original form, but sentences and paragraphs have sometimes been omitted, and a few verbal changes have been made in order that the pieces may be complete in themselves and contain no references to matter that originally preceded or followed them. In the selection and arrangement I owe much to the help and advice of three friends at the Press: Mr M. H. Black, Mr R. A. Becher, and Miss Anthea Roberts.

DAVID KNOWLES

PETERHOUSE
April 1961

CONTENTS

CONTENTS

LIST OF ILLUSTRATIONS

I

THE RULE OF SAINT BENEDICT

Benedict, called 'of Nursia' to distinguish him from other saints of the same name, was born c. 480 in Umbria (central Italy), and after beginning a normal education in Rome, escaped to lead a hermit's life near Subiaco. Here he founded and ruled a dozen small monasteries, but c. 520 abandoned his unruly monks and made a new settlement on Monte Cassino, between Rome and Naples. Here he wrote, or completed, his Rule and died, probably in 543.

FOR almost exactly a thousand years (530–1530) the social, cultural and religious life of Europe was deeply influenced by the monastic order and by the religious orders that were to a greater or less degree offshoots of or reversions to the original monastic ideal. For five of those centuries (530–1000) monasteries of a single type, the traditional Benedictine type, predominated and formed the reservoirs of literature, learning and spirituality for their world. Then, for a century and a half (1000–1153), coinciding in part with the great movement of reform that takes its name from Pope Gregory VII, the monastic ideal, both in its traditional form and in several new and more austere versions such as the Carthusian and the Cistercian, became identified with the perfection of the Christian life and flooded out over Europe. In this period many of the notable bishops and popes, and almost all the writers, were monks, and the movement culminated in the decades from 1120 to 1150 in which the Cistercians and their spokesman, St Bernard, dominated the life of the whole Western Church and built the abbeys whose remains or ruins are a familiar sight in every land. There followed another two centuries (1153–1349) in which the new orders of friars and canons, who combined at least a part of the monastic ideal with an apostolic or pastoral vocation, outshone the monks and gradually supplanted them as an intellectual and spiritual force. Finally, for the last two centuries of the medieval age (1350–1530) both monks, canons and friars, reduced in numbers and zeal, remained as preachers, theologians and landowners and were to all appearances an essential part of society until in the cataclysm of the Reformation they were swept away from the countries of Western and North-western Europe.

The men who figure in these pages are for the most part monks, though a few are friars and two owe their presence principally to their outspoken criticism of the monks or friars. It may not be out of place, therefore, to introduce their portraits by a short account of the Rule of St Benedict, which most of them professed to follow, and which was, and still is, the monastic code *par excellence* in the Western Church.

Seldom has so great a reputation as that of St Benedict rested on so small a base; rarely has so short a document as his Rule wielded such power. St Benedict owes his position in history to a single slim volume containing perhaps twelve thousand words, of which at least half help to form quotations from Scripture or liturgical directions. He was certainly a man with a reputation for wisdom and sanctity, and, if we may trust St Gregory the Great, he had great fame as a spiritual master and wonder-worker in the central Italy of his day. Yet had he written no Rule he would mean no more to us than do other men of sanctity and contemporary fame, such as his friend St Germanus of Capua, or our own Columbas and Aidans and Cuthberts of a later century. And as for Rules, others also, famous in their day and with a repute as masters, wrote them: Caesarius of Arles, for example, and the Irish St Columbanus. In what, then, does the unusual excellence of St Benedict's Rule consist?

A simple answer, and one that is true within limits, is to say the Rule is a document which can hold the attention of even a casual reader in the twentieth century, and one from which any reader may easily learn much of profit. I have written elsewhere of a public man of the present day, a member of no Church, who kept a copy in the desk of his office, and read the appointed portion every morning before beginning the day's work. On a first reading, indeed, the Rule may seem legalistic and even harsh, but this is a characteristic of all disciplinary or liturgical directories, from college or camp regulations upwards. What is unique in the Rule is its emphasis on much more than this, and here the Rule is quite literally unique, for we can search in vain for an exact parallel among all the Rules and directories, ancient and modern, from the Rule of St Basil the Great to that of St John Bosco in the nineteenth century. Perhaps the only apparent exception is the Rule of St Francis, and there the additions to the formal parts are exhortations and sentences of Scripture rather than wise and humane advice concerning every aspect of community life.

To understand the historical reasons for the success of the Rule we must take a somewhat wider view of the history of monasticism and of the social and economic circumstances of the age. Monasticism, considered as a recognized way of life distinct at once from that of the clergy and that of the devout Christian layfolk, was a spontaneous growth in Egypt, Syria and Asia Minor resulting from the newly won freedom of the Church, and perhaps also from the moral and psychological decadence of imperial society. Though all attempts to derive Christian monasticism from Jewish, Persian or Indian sources have failed, the two underlying aims of self-perfection, ascetical and mystical, are the outcome of fundamental desires which reappear in different forms throughout the history of mankind. The peculiarly Christian contributions were, on the

3

higher or deeper level, the love of Christ, the Son of God, as a living Person, imitable and attainable as a friend, and on the external plane, the incorporation of the monastic state, with its acceptance of the evangelical counsels, as an organized way of life within the Church.

The Egyptian and Syrian monachism passed with great rapidity through many stages of development, and in a little over a century had given to the Church, at least in germ, almost all the varieties of life possible—the strictly remote life of the hermit, the life of prayer in a retired community, and the life of studious or charitable work; while the great solitaries of the desert had handed down to Cassian the principles of the contemplative life which even St John of the Cross did no more than elaborate. Pachomius and Basil and others, by their Rules and Maxims, had put together a great body of practical and administrative wisdom from which later ages have never ceased to draw. Even such institutions as general chapters, unions of abbeys and regular visitations, often regarded as the creation of Cluny and Cîteaux, existed in a recognizable form in the East and directly influenced the reformers of the eleventh century.

This Eastern monasticism passed to the West during the early manhood of St Augustine and spread fairly rapidly. It assumed almost at once two forms—the one a pure imitation of the strict and often eremitical ideal of Egypt; the other a very much milder imitation of some of its features by families of clergy living round a bishop or great church. The latter stream, seen clearly for a moment in the group gathered round St Augustine at Thagaste and Hippo, disappeared underground for some centuries to emerge again as the canonical life of medieval and modern times. The former, the strict version, developed in Italy and Gaul and still more in Ireland, whence it was reimported into continental Europe by St Columbanus and others; this Celtic monasticism, besides many other peculiarities, was of great physical severity, with an elaborate penal code. Meanwhile, throughout Italy the eremitical and sequestered life developed, and monks and hermits of one kind or another were numerous, as can be seen clearly from the *Dialogues* of St Gregory. Regarded as a whole, however, this monastic movement had two great disabilities— it was unorganized and highly individualistic, and hence often extravagant, irregular and unsuccessful; while in its best manifestations it was too physically severe for the Western climate and Western temperaments.

At the same time the chaos into which Italy and Gaul were falling was beginning to threaten all Christian institutions. The monasteries of the East had drawn their recruits largely from a sophisticated, wealthy society; those of the West were most flourishing in districts where Christianity was established in peace. Now the northern invasions and the separation of East and West threatened to dissolve all.

It was at this crisis, which was probably not perceived by him as a crisis at all, that Benedict appeared. He had lived first as a hermit, then as the chosen head of small bodies of monks, and finally as the revered father of a large monastic family of his own foundation, and had himself suffered from the practical consequences of a lawless, changing society of monks, and he wrote his Rule either as a memorial of his teaching for his own sons or as a code at the command of high authority. Whatever the precise occasion, the Rule in fact gave for the first time a sane, workable directory governing every aspect of the life of a religious family—precise, concrete, eminently practical, serving at once to inspire and to control. The Rule thus—not as planned in Benedict's mind, or conceived as spiritual teaching, but as we see it in history— achieved a twofold end. It saved the monasticism of the East for the Roman Church, and it gave to Western Europe a religious and economic unit with a very high power of resistance and a great reserve of energy.

St Benedict, as has been truly said, is one of the last of the Romans, more truly Roman in spirit than even Gregory the Great. The impression of sanity, of strength, of moderation and of stability—typical qualities of the noblest Romans—is not merely subjective; it is noteworthy that in such a short document as the Rule the word *gravitas* (dignity) occurs five times, *rationabilis* (reasonable) and its adverb five times, *imperium* (authority) six times, *stabilis* and *stabilitas* (steadfast) six times, and *mensura* and *mensurate* (measure, moderation) ten times. This sense of strong government, of stability and yet of moderation, was precisely the quality most needed in one who was to hand down the wisdom of the desert to a new, adolescent, uncultivated age of shifting landmarks and peoples. It is a notable circumstance that wandering, lawless monks, so common a feature in Byzantine history and not unknown in the Italy of St Benedict's day, disappear as a class during the monastic centuries, and reappear only in the tragic breakdown of the Franciscan ideal at the end of the thirteenth century.

If St Benedict thus translated the past into a language which the present and future could understand, he was also able to base his spiritual fabric on a material foundation of great strength and simplicity. During his lifetime and for a century after, all the overhead organization of the Western Empire—political, social, economic, material; government, finances, public security, trade and roads—was going to pieces. All was tending to fall apart, in greater or less degree, into the smallest possible self-supporting units. Such a unit, such a cell, was the monastery of the Rule. Economically, spiritually, functionally it was self-supporting. Within the walls were all things necessary for its life—'the monastery, if possible, should be so constructed that all things needful, such as water, a mill, a garden, provision for domestic crafts, should be within its bounds' (ch. 66). This regulation, St Benedict goes on to say, will remove from the monks the need to go abroad, for this is gravely harmful to their souls '*quia omnino non expedit animabus eorum*', but here, as with so much in the Rule, the spiritual advantage carried with it others of a material and social kind.

Monasteries of this type, especially those in Mediterranean lands where the trinity of wheat, vine and olive could be cultivated within a single ring-fence, almost within a single enclosure, were vulnerable only at the hands of an armed force moved by a deliberate design to exterminate the whole community. All other forms of higher organization might dissolve, whether in empire, province or diocese, but this family would survive.

The economic unit was also a social unit. St Benedict's monastery is not, like the early Egyptian monasteries or the later reformed monasteries, the home of an *élite* of a single type. It is a family made up of every kind of vocation and every age of life—the priest, the cleric, the educated recruit, the peasant and the ex-serf, and, below all, children of every age and class committed to God by their parents. All these, once they have reached their fifteenth year, take the order in which they entered the monastery, save for the service of the altar.

Finally, on the level of discipline and organization the Rule is streamlined. Principles are laid down, and a few key points are established, but no machinery that needs to be watched, repaired or replaced. There is no essential or permanent connection of any kind with any person or body outside the monastery. The abbot is elected by his monks, and then has full patriarchal power, limited only by humanity, sane reason, the Rule and the law of God. There are two kinds of simplicity —the formless, colourless simplicity which is the process of deprivation and negation, and the supreme simplicity which contains within itself in an eminent degree a multiplicity of qualities. The simplicity of the Rule is of the latter class; it has its dangers, as will be seen, but such a craft, streamlined and with no top-hamper, was infinitely better fitted to ride the heavy seas of the dark ages than would have been the complicated constitutions of the later Middle Ages.

St Benedict founded no order; he did not even send out from Monte Cassino a succession of colonies; he lived with and for his relatively small community of the hill; he left them the memory of a holy life and the codex of the Rule. The influence of that Rule on the religious and cultural life of the West was enormous. It was never imposed as a code; there was no order to grow from a mustard-seed as did Cîteaux in later centuries. The Rule supplanted other rules or gained a foothold alongside of them simply by reason of its intrinsic excellence and practicability; it gradually came to colour the whole of Western monachism as a powerful chemical ingredient might gradually colour and saturate a liquid. It was not till the heyday of Cluny that the idea became current that all monks were a *familia S. Benedicti*, with a single patriarch; not till 1215 were the autonomous houses of Europe loosely joined in provincial chapters; not till *c.* 1400 were black monks known as Benedictines; and not till the last decade of the nineteenth century were all Benedictines united in the loosest of confederations.

Yet for all that the Rule is one of the basic documents of the Middle Ages. As such it lay behind all houses of monks from the age of Charlemagne onwards, as also behind the majority of nunneries. Later, when the new orders began to rise in the eleventh century, the Rule was there also as the basic code. Thus it was behind the Camaldolese, and Vallombrosans, as also behind the various movements such as Tiron, Savigny and Cîteaux; later still it was the code of the Silvestrines and the Olivetans. Even the hermit Carthusians took much from it. But it was also the type-Rule in a still wider sense. When Canon Law was formed piece by piece, and later codified by Gratian, himself a Camaldolese monk, and others in the twelfth century, the Rule was taken for all monastic matters as a document on a level with decretals and councils, and thus such portions as the election of an abbot, corporate ownership and personal poverty, the vows and noviciate were taken up into canon law as the Church's own utterances. Similarly, a number of liturgical details passed from the Rule into common use, such as the addition of Compline to the other Hours, while some of the arrangements of the time-table, such as the *Summum Silentium* from Compline to Prime, became part of the common heritage of all religious orders. The Rule even gave to almost all European languages the term collation in the sense of light repast, a direct if distant descendant of the nightly reading in St Benedict's monastery of the *Conferences* or *Collations* of Cassian, and probably also the word chapter in the sense of a meeting of monks or clergy.

But the Rule had a still wider and more beneficent influence on the West. For many centuries almost all the writers and very many of the most distinguished bishops and royal councillors and administrators were monks, who had heard every day, year in year out, a section of the Rule read in chapter, and had learnt much of it by heart as the guide of their lives. We could be sure, even if we had not the evidence of countless quotations, explicit or hidden, that the Rule was ever present in their conscious or sub-conscious mind. We can scarcely be wrong in supposing that the peculiar qualities of the Rule—its simplicity, its moderation, its humanity—must have moulded their outlook and judgment, and through them, the outlook and judgment of countless individuals in the higher levels of thought and action throughout the centuries that have been called Benedictine.

The Rule is full of maxims for those in power, as anyone will agree who read the two chapters (II and LXIV) instructing the abbot: 'Let him always put mercy before judgment, that he may find mercy himself—let him not be jealous or suspicious for so he will never have peace—let him strive rather to be loved than to be feared—let him be prudent in his correction, lest while he strive to scour off the rust, he break the vessel—let him realize what a difficult task he has undertaken, that of directing souls and adapting himself to many varied characters.' It would be hard to find more practical wisdom, always humane but never weak, pressed into such small compass. Nor are these the only chapters; that on the cellarer is another masterpiece of good sense, while what could be more generous than the opening of the short chapter (XXXVI) on the aged and children: 'Although our human nature is of itself moved to gentleness with the aged and with children, yet the authority of the Rule should take thought for them too', and the no less magnificent opening of chapter XXXVI: 'Before all else and above all else must come the care of the sick, so that the service may be rendered to them which is in truth rendered to Christ, for he said, "I was sick and ye visited me," and "What ye have done to one of these little ones ye have done to me".' Examples could be multiplied, such as the *licet legamus* passages, where he mitigates the old prohibitions and achievements of the desert, and the celebrated phrases of lapidary brevity in which he speaks of the chapel: '*oratorium hoc sit quod dicitur, nec ibi quidquid aliud geratur aut condatur'* (LII)[1] and of those who would pray there—'*simpliciter intrent et orent'*.[2]

But it is not isolated maxims so much as the whole spirit of the Rule that strikes the mind: a spirit of trust in human nature aided by grace; the utterance of a man who, after long and often bitter experience of human weakness and malice, still firmly believed that men could become true sons of God and in so doing could help others to go with them; that the truth spoken with patience and love was a better instrument than dragooning or punishment; and that the eternal fact of God's existence as a Father and Judge was a more potent motive and sanction than any system of legal checks and threats.

[1] 'Let the oratory be what its name implies (i.e. a place of prayer), and let nothing else be done or put there.' The precept is taken from the Rule of St Augustine, but its expression is perfected by St Benedict.

[2] 'Let them go straight in and pray.'

II

BEDE THE VENERABLE

Bede, known as the Venerable (673–735), entered the monastery of Jarrow, on the south bank of the Tyne near Newcastle, as a child, and remained to become a professed monk. He wrote many theological and 'scientific' works in Latin, and also the 'Church History of England', for which he is principally celebrated. He also translated the gospels and wrote verse in his native tongue. He was one of the chief ornaments of the brief but brilliant Northumbrian cultural epoch of which many relics remain—the church of Jarrow itself, the Lindisfarne Gospels, the Codex Amiatinus of the New Testament and the treasures of St Cuthbert's tomb.

BEDE THE VENERABLE is the first great Englishman of whom we can form a clear personal picture. The early kings and missionaries and the great men of the generation before Bede, St Chad of Lichfield, St Wilfrid of York, St Cuthbert of Lindisfarne, are either dim figures or are known to us only as Bede himself saw and described them. But of Bede we have not only his many writings to reveal his personality, but also a sketch of his character and of his last days drawn by an intimate disciple, and the person revealed in all these sources is one and the same, a clear-cut, living and very attractive being.

Bede lived near the Northumbrian coast, on what to an Italian or a Gaul must have seemed the very fringe of the world. The only sea he knew was the grey sea over which his forefathers had sailed to Britain, and on which the long ships of the Vikings were soon to appear. He lived also in the darkest hour of European civilization, when the last traces of the Roman organization had gone, and when both the Eastern Empire and the Western kingdoms were threatened by the vast pincer movement of the Moslem advance. In the east Moslem fleets and armies were at the gates of Constantinople; in the west their cavalry was debouching into Aquitaine from the passes of the Pyrenees. During Bede's lifetime East and West alike were saved by two of the decisive battles of the world; in 718, while he was writing his commentary on the Scriptures, Islam was beaten off the walls of Constantinople; in 732, when he had finished his writing, Charles Martel destroyed the Moslem army on the field of Tours. Whether Bede knew of all this and appreciated it we do not know; all we know is that away in the north he was preserving for his own world and for us the history of our common ancestors and our common faith.

Externally, Bede's life was remarkably uneventful. He was born in 672 near Jarrow, and brought up as a child in the monastery there which had been recently founded. 'From the which time', to use his own words, 'I spent all the days of my life in the said monastery, applying all my study to the meditation of holy scripture: and observing withal the regular discipline, and keeping the daily singing of God's service in the church, the rest of my life I was delighted always to learn of others, and to teach myself or else to write.' At Jarrow, indeed, or in the neighbouring sister-house of Wearmouth, he spent the whole of his life till he died, sixty-three years old, in 735. He probably never went further south than York, nor further north than Lindisfarne. It was an uneventful life and an undistinguished life: Bede never became a bishop, nor even an abbot; and he never met or influenced directly the rulers of Church or State. Even his undoubted holiness was unobtrusive. He wrote of the wonders worked by others, but none are recorded of him. He described the conversion of England, but he probably never preached to anyone outside his monastery.

Why then do we remember him and consider him great? The men of his own age would have said: 'Because of his great learning and science.' Bede had, undoubtedly, a mind of extraordinary grasp and he was perhaps the most learned man of his age. Living on the edge of the world, in a land with no tradition of learning and converted to Christianity only half a century before, he had no books save for the collection that had been assembled by his first abbot, Benet Biscop. It was a collection that contained most of the works, theological, scriptural, scientific and literary that had been filtered down, either by accident or design, from the legacy of the Roman Empire, but so far as bulk went, it was only two hundred volumes or so strong. Yet with this collection Bede made himself the most learned man in Western Europe. What is more, he controlled and focused his learning so as to make something of it that has endured to our own day. He taught himself to write Latin accurately and fluently, and in that Latin he wrote commentaries on the gospels which were ranked with those of St Augustine and St Gregory the Great. Pages from them passed into the Roman and monastic breviaries, and ever since to the present day they have been read on appointed days by priests in every part of the world. Bede is the only Englishman who has been saluted by the whole Western world as one of the Doctors of the Church. He also mastered the mathematics and astronomy of his day and for centuries his books remained the classical authority for Europe on matters of chronology. Here again we feel his influence today, for it was Bede who resolutely adopted and thus made fashionable the dating of years by the Christian era. But all this would have done no more than to make him an interesting historical figure. What makes him real and living to us is his last work, the history of the Church in England from the earliest times to his own day, together with the shorter lives of St Cuthbert and of his own abbots. He is, indeed, the father of English history. But for him, early English history would be largely a matter of archaeology and bare dates, eked out by a few charters and laws. More than this, Bede is a great historian, perhaps the greatest between the last notable historian of the ancient world and those of the Italian renaissance. The pains he took to acquire and check reliable information, to secure genuine documents, and to criticize and present all this, the care he took to have it read and revised before finally giving it to the world, would be admirable in the most scholarly historian of today.

And yet these qualities are not by themselves those which make Bede what he is to us. The quiet monk of Jarrow is also a human being. He is an Englishman, and the first Englishman to declare himself a lover of England not by patriotic phrases, but in his desire to tell how England became Christian and of the cloud of witnesses that had so quickly made this island an island of saints. He was, beyond this, a born presenter of character, a true brother of the poet of Beowulf and of the writers of the great sagas of the North. Half-a-dozen of the best stories in English history come from Bede—the martyrdom of St Alban, the arrival of St Augustine, the story of Cuthbert the shepherd boy or the hermit of Farne warmed by the seals, the story of Hilda and the poet Caedmon. And for character also: all that we know of the kings of Mercia and Northumbria, of Wilfrid of York, of the abbots Benedict and Ceolfrid, and of many others, comes from Bede. If you pick Bede's book up, it is hard to put down. Let me give one or two perhaps unfamiliar examples of Bede's gift of narrative and characterization. He is writing of a hermit in Northumbria:

Since his cell stood upon a river's side, he was wont to dip and plunge himself in the flowing water oftentimes, and continue there singing of psalms as long as he could abide for cold, the water now and then coming up to his hips, and now and then to his chin. In the winter season, when pieces of ice half-broken dropped down on every side of him, which he had broken to plunge into the river, diverse men seeing him said; 'It is a marvellous matter and a strange case, brother Birthelm (for so he was called), that you can possibly suffer such bitter and sharp cold.' Whereupon he answered simply (for he was but a simple and sober-spirited man), 'I have known places colder than this.'

Here is another describing the last days of the nun, Tortgyd:

Now when Tortgyd had lived three years after the death of her Abbess Ethelburga, she was so far pined away with sickness that she could not only stir none of her limbs, but was speechless and could not move her tongue. In which case, as she lay, suddenly she opened her mouth and eyes and looking up to heaven began thus to speak. 'Thy coming to me is most joyful, and thou art heartily welcome.' And when she had so said, she held her peace a little, as it were abiding for an answer. And then, as it were a little angrily, she said again: 'I cannot gladly suffer this.' And straightway holding her peace a little, she spake the third time and said: 'If it may not by any means be today, I beseech thee that the mean time be not delayed.' Wherewith holding her peace a little as she had done before, she ended her talk thus: 'And if it be fully so appointed, and cannot be changed, I beseech thee that there be no more but only this next night between.' After which words, being demanded of them that sat about her, to whom she spake 'Forsooth,' quoth she, 'to my most dear mother Ethelburga.' And even as she made request, after one day and night passed, she was delivered both of the bond of the flesh and of her sickness and passed to God.

It is altogether fitting that Bede's own death should have had an eye-witness who had inherited his own powers of narrative. Bede, knowing that his hour was nigh, hoped for time to finish his translation of the gospel of St John:

And the aforesaid lad, whose name was Wilberch, said: 'Dear Master, there yet remains one sentence not written.' Whereupon he answered: 'Very well; do thou write it.' And after a little the lad said: 'Now it is written.' And Bede, 'Well indeed,' said he, 'finished it is; thou hast said the truth. Take my head between thy hands, since greatly I long to sit over against the holy place, in which I was wont to pray, so that I may sit and call upon my Father.' And so sitting on the pavement of his cell, and chanting 'Glory be to the Father, and to the Son, and to the Holy Ghost' he breathed forth his soul.

In his learning, in his candour, and in his art Bede is without rival in the Middle Ages. Among the world's great historians he has perhaps most kinship with the father of Greek history, Herodotus. There is the same reverence for the past, the same excellence in direct narrative and anecdote, the same deceptive appearance of *naïveté*, the same patriotism. If Herodotus is the richer in grasp, Bede has the clearer vision of his world and its purpose. But the reader of Bede quickly comes to feel that Bede himself is more admirable and lovable than any of his characters. Hard as we might find it to put into words, most of us would feel that there is a certain blend of qualities that is peculiarly English, and that throughout the ages this has been embodied again and again in great Englishmen. Of these embodiments Bede is the earliest and in some ways the purest instance. He is of the family of Alfred the Great, of Chaucer, of Thomas More and of Samuel Johnson. Shakespeare is too myriad-minded to be of any family, but he has Bede's qualities among the rest. There is no brilliance in Bede, but much steady clarity; no overtones and undertones, no subtle intuition, no twilight mystery, no lightning flash of genius. He lives and writes in noonday sunshine. If we search for a simile to fit him, we do not think of steel or diamond, of the opal or of quicksilver; rather, perhaps, we think of the mellow purity of gold. Simple, sane, loyal, trusting, warm-hearted, serious, with that ready sense of pathos which has always been a mark of English literature—these are not spectacular qualities, and they may easily degenerate into stolidity or sentimentality or mere good nature, or even into the ponderous or the ridiculous. In Bede they do none of these things because falsehood and vanity of any kind was quite foreign to him, and because Bede was a good man who, as he himself said, could live without shame and die without fear.

III

THREE MONASTIC FOUNDERS: DUNSTAN, ETHELWOLD AND OSWALD

St Dunstan (909–88), St Ethelwold (?910–84) and St Oswald (?925–92) worked together to restore to England the monastic life that had decayed or had been destroyed during the period of Scandinavian invasion. Among the abbeys founded or restored were Glastonbury (Somerset), Abingdon (Berkshire) and Ramsey (Huntingdonshire), while monks were also established in the cathedral priories of Winchester and Worcester. Elsewhere monasteries and nunneries multiplied rapidly. Dunstan became bishop in turn of Worcester, London and Canterbury; Ethelwold of Winchester; and Oswald of Worcester and York.

ETHELWOLD's biographer, Aelfric, who knew him intimately, gives us a vivid picture of his energy in his last years in constructing and visiting the monasteries he had founded, most of which lay far from Winchester, in translating books into English—among them, the Rule of St Benedict for nuns —and in teaching his young disciples. His physical sufferings were great, but he spared himself not at all, nor departed from the monastic Rule in regard to food. He left behind him a reputation for austerity and severity, but also of fatherly care and sympathy for the unfortunate and the oppressed; the records of his life show him a lover of the chant and a skilled craftsman, and the Benedictional in the British Museum which bears his name stands as a monument to his patronage of the art in which his countrymen excelled. In his last days he was visited and counselled by Dunstan, and a fortunate accident has left us with an eye-witness's account of the meeting, at which, in the presence of monks from both the Winchester houses, their founder and bishop ratified an agreement of union and concord between them.

Dunstan died four years later, in 988. His last years had been given almost wholly to the pastoral care of his diocese and to the direct service of God. From the many living touches of his earliest biographer a very real portrait of this great and eminently holy man emerges, though the traits are so many and so minute that a reader can scarcely analyse the whole for himself, still less transmit the impression to others. The sympathetic, receptive nature which in his early manhood made him the friend and guide of so many varied characters, the unshakable strength of his later years which made him to the end the master even of Ethelwold, the wisdom and states-manship which enabled him to be the counsellor and friend of successive kings and one of the creators of a united England, the gift of artistic creation of the highest order which is perhaps the most remarkable of all his gifts, and, finally, the mature sanctity which in his later years transcended and superseded his other activities and characteristics—all these, revealed to us in this way or that, make of Dunstan a figure of singular attractiveness, whose final and lasting impression is one, not of brilliance and fire, but of a calm and mellow light. His final illness came upon him shortly after Mass, at which he had preached thrice, on the feast of the Ascension, a season already associated in the memories of Englishmen with the last moments of the Venerable Bede. He lingered till the Saturday morning of 19 May when, immediately after receiving Viaticum at a Mass celebrated in his presence, he passed away. His last words, according to a tradition which has every claim to belief, were those of the Psalmist: 'The merciful and gracious Lord hath made a remembrance of His marvellous works; He hath given food to them that fear Him.'

PLATE I

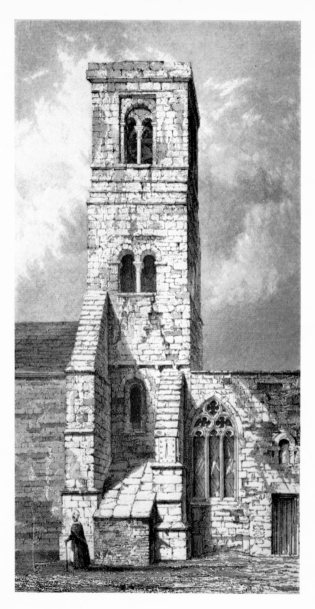

JARROW

PLATE II

ST DUNSTAN

Oswald, the youngest, survived till 992. His memory has fared well in subsequent ages, partly because his supposedly greater gentleness and moderation have been contrasted with the more violent methods of his colleagues. Actually we have few details out of which to form his portrait. A Dane by blood, physically robust and with a magnificent voice, he does not seem to have shared the artistic gifts of Ethelwold and Dunstan, though his career at Fleury and his reception of Abbo at Ramsey are evidence that he shared their love of learning. Like Ethelwold, he was tireless in visiting his monasteries in Mercia and the fens, but it is as bishop and father of his people that he stands out in the pages of his biographer. Though archbishop of York for twenty years, Worcester was always the church of his predilection; it is with its land that his name is linked, and there he died, as he had wished.

In November 991 he paid a notable visit, which he knew would be his last, to Ramsey. It was an annual custom for Oswald and Aethelwine, the founder, to meet there as guests, and the writer of the archbishop's life, who was present, gives a vivid and interesting description of the scene in the abbey during Oswald's Mass on this occasion, and of the banquet, given by Aethelwine, that followed it. Two days later Oswald took leave of the monks, after asking their blessing and bestowing his own, with a prayer that they might all meet in heaven. He spent the winter months at Worcester, in ordinary health; and entered upon the season of Lent and the beginning of spring, a time always precious to him, with all his ordinary practices. Among these it was his custom to wash the feet of twelve poor men daily. On the last morning of his life, which was also the last day of February, he accomplished his usual task, reciting as he did so the Gradual Psalms. When, at the end, all knelt before the crucifix for the doxology, the archbishop's spirit passed away.

The memory of the three great bishops was cherished by their countrymen. The records of those who had known them show that they received at once the veneration of all classes; a century later we can find Wulfstan of Worcester, at a crisis of his own career, seeking strength in the example given by his two saintly predecessors; fifty years later again William of Malmesbury, with that true sense of values that underlies his superficial lack of discrimination, devotes to them words of reverent admiration such as he reserves for the greatest alone. They and their work, however, have failed to receive due recognition in modern times, for while the generality of English historians of religion have allowed themselves to be wholly occupied with the Norman monasticism and the *éclat* of Lanfranc and Anselm, the romantic school of writers on monastic history has turned more readily to the previous centuries of Aidan, Wilfrid, Aldhelm, Bede and Boniface; moreover, the darkness of the ninth century has in the past been rendered still more treacherous by the pages of the pseudo-Asser and the pseudo-Ingulf, so that the absolute break between old and new has not been adequately realized. When the strong new life of monastic England in the reigns of Edgar and Ethelred is seen in a true light, the achievement of the three, and especially of Ethelwold and Dunstan, can be more justly assessed. As has been said, they left no new impress on the form of monastic life; they changed nothing, nor did they enrich the blood of the religious world by their writings or spiritual doctrine. But in another respect they did everything: they called the dead to life; they created a great and flourishing system upon vacant soil; and to Dunstan especially, as to Augustine of Canterbury before him, are due in a very real sense the titles of patron and father of the monks of medieval England.

IV

LANFRANC

Lanfranc (? 1005–89), a Lombard by birth, went north and taught theology at Avranches. Becoming a monk at Bec in Normandy, he continued to teach Scripture and theology, and was regarded as the greatest master of Western Europe. Among his pupils was the young Anselm. Lanfranc became the trusted counsellor of Duke William of Normandy who appointed him abbot of Caen and, after the Conquest, archbishop of Canterbury in 1070. He remained till his death counsellor and agent of the Conqueror, and reorganized the English Church.

FROM the very beginning of his reign William the Conqueror began the task of reorganizing the whole Church in England on the model of Normandy. He appointed a number of Normans to vacant abbacies and remodelled the episcopate with the aid of papal legates. For a moment he had thoughts of giving Cluny a leading part in the new life, and applied to the abbot, St Hugh, for a dozen of his best men. Hugh declined to furnish them; it was not part of Cluny's policy. Thrown back thus upon his own resources, the Conqueror summoned from Caen the man who had for some years been his trusted adviser and whom, in the very year of the Conquest, he had made abbot of his own foundation of St Stephen's. From Lanfranc's arrival in England in 1070 till his death in 1089 his was the paramount influence in the monastic world of England. It is therefore necessary to form some idea of his character and policy, the more so because this great man has suffered a certain neglect at the hands of historians, who have devoted their attention almost exclusively to the Conqueror or to Anselm, and in so far as they have treated of Lanfranc, it has been as statesman and ecclesiastic rather than as monk and spiritual leader.

Lanfranc came to the monastic life comparatively late, and with a character and a mind already formed and exercised. We should, therefore, be justified in supposing, even if we had not the whole tenor and flavour of his acts and utterances to guide us, that he remained to the end, both as monk and prelate, distinguishable from one who had spent all his years from childhood or boyhood in the cloister. If the traditional date of his birth is correct, he was at least thirty-five when, after a successful career in law at Pavia, he left Italy and came to Normandy, where he taught at Avranches and attracted numerous pupils. Dissatisfied with this life, he resolved to turn to solitude and obscurity, and chose Bec, then in its infancy, as the monastery most likely to provide him with both. For three years he lived there unknown; then, for whatever reason, the life ceased to please him and he decided to leave Bec and become a hermit. Herluin discovered his intention, and persuaded him to abandon it; it is impossible to be certain what took place between them, but the moment was decisive alike for Bec and for Lanfranc. He gave up wholly his desire for a solitary life, became immediately prior of Bec and opened a school there in which he taught all comers, among them several of the most influential churchmen of the next generation, one of them being the future Alexander II. The story of his growing fame, of his share in the condemnation of Berengarius, of his opposition to William's marriage in 1058 and of the subsequent reconciliation by which he became his intimate counsellor, is part of the history of Europe and need not concern us here. It is more important to seize some of the traits of Lanfranc's firm and energetic character.

Wisdom was the quality that seemed most to distinguish Lanfranc in the eyes of his contemporaries, and by wisdom they perhaps understood that elevation of mind and calm foresight which enabled him to impose order upon men and institutions, for great as was his reputation as theologian even his own age realized that his disciples, rather than his writings, were his best monument. Yet we cannot read his letters, with their short, lucid, decisive sentences and their sane, masculine judgments, without submitting to his mental power. Out of the strong could come forth sweetness, as we can see if we care to read his letters to Anselm at Bec or to his monk nephews, but strength was dominant even in his love. There is something Roman in his character and mind; a clarity, an order, a keenness, a granite strength. As a young man, his agility of thought and speech had won him many victories, and even in later life the brilliant ultramontane used his gifts at the expense of the duller Normans. This characteristic, and the manner of his endeavour to quit Bec, show that the natural man remained long in Lanfranc; we may perhaps detect in more than one of his actions as archbishop a prudence of this world that contrasts with the direct candour and simplicity of Anselm. Yet his relations in late life with his aged abbot, his avoidance of all display when he revisited Bec, and the affection with which he was regarded by the children of the cloister, combine to show that by self-discipline he had made mellow what was harsh. Gilbert Crispin, who knew him intimately, speaks of his loving-kindness, and we have the most weighty testimony to his benignity at Christ Church, Canterbury, and to the fatherly care with which he ruled his English monks. He noticed at once if one was sad, spoke to him immediately and elicited the reason. It was by love, not by force, that he accomplished the necessary reforms, for he was a most skilled ruler of the hearts of men. Eadmer, who as a child and young monk had known him well, gives us details at first hand of Lanfranc's delicacy and generosity. He never suffered parents of his monks to want, and was accustomed to give them assistance by the hands of their children. There is a touching story of one such mother and her son— it may well have been Eadmer himself—and of the great archbishop sitting in the cloister and noting the monk's sorrow. Such incidents speak for themselves; if we wish confirmation, we may find it in Malmesbury's eloquent praise of the community of Christ Church as a living memorial of Lanfranc's charity and devotion, or in the words used by an anonymous English chronicler to note the final departure of the venerable father and protector of all monks.

It has, indeed, been hinted by more than one recent historian that Lanfranc's monasticism was only a phase of his life, which passed from his mind when he became immersed in the high problems of a statesman; such a view is hard to reconcile with his actions or with what is told us by Eadmer, and we need not doubt the sincerity of the archbishop's own words, when, writing to Alexander II, he speaks of the life in the monastery as that which he holds dearest in the world. Lanfranc and Anselm differ much in character and mind, the one energetic, realistic, mastering every new task that is put upon him, the other gentle, excelling in speculation, remaining his calm, consistent self amid the rough chaos of events, but it is clear from the letters which they exchanged that in their conception of the monastic life they were at one. As a young man, Lanfranc must have been familiar with the kind of life advocated by Romuald and Peter Damian, and the vision of a hermit's life remained with him during his first years at Bec. That was not his vocation, nor would he have been drawn to the life of Cluny as it was brought to fullest development. His ideal was the Bec he had helped to create: a regular, liturgical life, with scope for study, and with the duty of raising the standard of religious life both by teaching and, when need arose, by going out to govern. This policy he developed as archbishop; the monasteries were to be the great powers in reorganizing the spiritual life of England, and he drew unsparingly upon Bec and Caen when he needed men for bishoprics, abbacies and for the good of Christ Church. In his conception of the monastic life, Lanfranc thus held something of a *via media* between the reformers of Italy and the tendency in England before the Conquest. He wished for a strict, ordered, cloistered monasticism, but not for one wholly separated by physical barriers from the life of the rest of the Church. Nowhere, perhaps, is his mind more clearly seen than in his organization and extension of the cathedral monasteries.

This monastic policy suited exactly the needs and situation of the Norman and English Churches as they were under the Conqueror: national churches, controlled with a very real, though undefined, power by a monarch anxious for reform. It was the exact counterpart of Lanfranc's attitude as primate, in which again he held in practice to a *via media*. With the full Gregorian programme of centralized and direct government from Rome, which implied a reduction of the jurisdiction of metropolitans, the possibility of all cases going on appeal to the Pope, and the growing exemption of monasteries from episcopal control, he had little practical sympathy. He had left Italy before the reformed papacy had begun to take the lead in the reform of the Church, and in Normandy, where the Emperor was unknown and where simony, at least under William I, was non-existent, the ideal condition of things appeared to be a strong hierarchy under a powerful primate and powerful king. In England, as in Normandy, regeneration was to be effected by the example and influence of the monks.

The great archbishop died on 24 May 1089, after a short illness and with his mind clear to the last, as he had always hoped. Despite his extreme old age, he had been active till the last, as is seen by the leading part he took in the proceedings against William of St Carilef in the spring of 1087. More than fifty years had passed since the young, but already celebrated teacher had arrived in the valley of Bec, and during that half-century Lanfranc had shown his consummate ability in adapting himself to the most varied needs and circumstances, and in remaining always a dominant figure, whether as the foremost doctor of Europe against Berengarius, or the representative of Norman monasticism, or the reorganizer of the English Church, or the principal upholder of the Conqueror's *régime* in England. Yet he remains in the end something of an enigmatic figure to us, not by reason of any complexity of character or change of policy, for throughout all his actions the strong, direct, realist mind is apparent, but because even with all the material at our disposal it is not easy to make a single, living whole or to reconcile the various estimates of his contemporaries with each other and with his character as revealed by his actions and his correspondence. The vicegerent of William at Norwich, the energetic opponent of St Carilef, the archbishop who deferred to the Conqueror's opinion on more than one occasion seems at times a different man from the devoted friend of Herluin and Anselm, and the kindly father of the childhood's memories of Eadmer. We cannot fail to miss in Lanfranc that simplicity of outlook, that single aim, that is reflected in every recorded action and word of Anselm, and it is hard in the last resort to avoid the conclusion that in the realm of the pure intellect Lanfranc had agility and versatility rather than depth and intuition; that in the art of government he was a supremely able administrator and organizer of the plans and needs of the moment rather than a creative genius who could keep his eyes fixed upon the lodestar of a single end; and that on the deepest plane of the spirit, for all the strength of his religious conviction and his real nobility of soul, he remained an ecclesiastic dependent upon and moved by the changing, temporary circumstances of the time rather than a saint who, with whatever limitations of mental outlook, directs his every action to the forwarding of a kingdom not of this world. It is certainly noteworthy that although recognized as such a dominant personality in the Europe of his day, neither in the sphere of learning, nor in the monastic life, nor in high ecclesiastical policy did Lanfranc anticipate or direct the minds of men to the ideas that were to be the moulding forces of the near future.

But though Lanfranc was essentially a man of his age, whereas Anselm is for all time, there can be no doubt which of the two had the greater influence upon the framework of the Church in England. Though the two widest of Lanfranc's aims—the subjection of all sees in the British Isles to Canterbury, and the direct and uncontrolled government of his province by the metropolitan primate—failed of realization, the one because of its inherent impracticability, the other by reason of the victory of Gregorian ideas, it may be doubted whether of all the eminent men who filled the see of Canterbury between Augustine and Cranmer any individual, save only Theodore of Tarsus, had a greater share than Lanfranc in organizing the Church in this country. And as the propagator of the monastic order in England and of its conversion to the Norman model he holds a place among the archbishops which only Dunstan can challenge. When he died, every important abbey in England was held by a Norman, the Norman architecture, observance and economic system were everywhere taking root, the number of monastic houses had increased by a half, the number of monks in the country had probably more than doubled, and the monasteries as a whole had entered the feudal system. For all this Lanfranc, under

William, was very largely responsible. He was, in a very real sense, the 'father of monks'. His letters that survive can be but a fraction of his correspondence, but they show him with a solicitude for all the churches, defending the monasteries against unjust aggression, overseeing nunneries, counselling abbots, and watching over the interests of private individuals. Here indeed he held a position without parallel among the archbishops throughout the centuries. No other, not even Dunstan, had such universal powers of surveillance and control; neither before nor after did any individual so regulate the affairs of houses and persons among the black monks until, in other circumstances and for other ends, powers still greater were entrusted to the King's Vicar-general, Thomas Cromwell.

V

ANSELM OF CANTERBURY

St Anselm (1033–1109), born at Aosta, crossed the Alps in search of learning and became Lanfranc's pupil and a monk of Bec, of which house he became the second abbot. Appointed against his will archbishop of Canterbury by William II (Rufus) in 1093, he was twice in exile in support of the papal claims. The most eminent thinker and theologian of his age, his is the first great name in the history of scholastic thought.

ST ANSELM has a double title to celebrity. On the one hand, he is one of the most saintly and attractive of medieval men, the single representative of the traditional Benedictine monachism of his age who can be said to rival St Bernard in spiritual and intellectual distinction. On the other hand, he is the only monk in the whole long history of monasticism who can claim a place among the very greatest thinkers of the world. Though as a statesman and leader of men he must take rank below Lanfranc, as a spiritual guide, as a father in God, and quite simply as a human being he reaches a higher level than his first master. He is one of the two or three men in the course of fourteen centuries who have seemed to come nearest to the Benedictine ideal. The Venerable Bede is another, and a composite character-photograph of the two would make any description of the type unnecessary. Bede, however, must needs have something of the archaic about him; he is unrepeatable. Anselm, on the other hand, could have walked as easily into S. Germain-des-prés in Mabillon's time as he might walk into Solesmes abbey today. Simplicity, humanity, gentleness allied to strength, a clear and sane mind, and a capacity to give and to receive love, are all distinguishing traits of the abbot of Bec. He was neither a leader nor a reformer nor a politician; he was a father, a thinker and a guide.

If a plebiscite were to be taken today among all Benedictines as to whom they would choose as the nearest approach in history to the ideal of an abbot as presented in the Rule of St Benedict, Anselm would surely head the poll by a comfortable majority. As a writer, he is one of that small group who win not only our admiration, but our personal affection. He was indeed a very lovable man. He himself tells us (and he should have known) that he was always beloved of all good men, and his contemporary biographer tells us that even William the Conqueror, usually so formidable, relaxed in Anselm's presence, not immune to the spell that he could cast and to that charm which, so his friend Eadmer tells us, was so strong as to resemble a physical force. Those who think of men of the eleventh century as savage, harsh and cruel should watch Anselm at the bedside of the monk Herewald, old, sick, and unable to take solid food. Him Anselm fed with grapejuice, crushing the fruit in his hand and so feeding the invalid, who refused all other food and drink. It was the same Anselm who advised an abbot who ruled the children of the cloister by terror and without success to try his own method—sympathy, patience, and affection. It may well be imagined that such a character, strong and firm, but also intuitive and receptive, was better able to work upon men as individuals than as groups of a society.

If Anselm as a monk is an almost perfect exemplar of a class, as a thinker he is a portent, a Melchizedek, without father or mother or genealogy. When he first came up from Aosta to learn from Lanfranc the great stirring of mental life, the intellectual adolescence of medieval Europe, was everywhere apparent in the cathedral schools of France, but the manifestations were no more than harbingers and promises of mature and creative thought. Lanfranc and Berengarius, the two most celebrated teachers of their day, are men of their day, who interest only the specialist historian. Anselm, on the other hand, is one of the half-dozen medieval thinkers who belong to the ages, who have permanently enriched the currents of thought. He is a portent because he has no predecessor; his master Lanfranc spoke with another tongue and on a lower level of power. Anselm himself, indeed, proclaimed with sincerity that Augustine was his master, and his language, certainly, as well as his approach, in which heart and mind, knowledge and love, run together as yoke-fellows, are unmistakably Augustinian. But his thought, and especially those elements in it that are most characteristic and most familiar, is derived from no master. Though his most celebrated signature-phrase, *fides quaerens intellectum*, is an echo of Augustine, the programme it implies is new, and the candid simplicity of daring with which Anselm, with reason alone as his guide, offers to sound and to explain some of the deepest problems of theology and philosophy, has nothing in it, save an occasional verbal reminiscence, of his pretended exemplar. Later philosophers, St Thomas among them, have said hard things of Anselm, but some of the ideas he put into currency, and in particular his well-known 'ontological' argument for the existence of God, have never ceased to appeal to a succession of great thinkers from Bonaventure to Descartes and Hegel. Anselm never taught in the schools; he would seem to have spoken only to a group of young monks at Bec or Canterbury, and then to have written down for them what he had said. He was in this a man of his age, and of a very brief age. Forty years earlier, no group of young monks would have been capable of appreciating such teaching; sixty years later, those capable and desirous of receiving it would not have been in a monastery. Anselm's Bec, which to us seems characteristic, was in fact exceptional even in Anselm's day, and the monastic world has never since seen its like.

VI

AILRED OF RIEVAULX

St Ailred (?1109–67), an Englishman born at Hexham, was educated at the court of the half-English King David I of Scotland, whose service he left to become a Cistercian monk at Rievaulx (Yorkshire, North Riding). Elected abbot of Revesby (Lincolnshire), a daughter house of Rievaulx, he was recalled to be abbot of his old home 1147–67. He wrote several works, historical, theological and spiritual, and was known as 'the Bernard of the North'.

AILRED OF RIEVAULX, the 'Bernard of the North', is a singularly attractive figure whom, thanks to the records left by a disciple and still more to his own writings, we can see as a living man in some completeness. No other English monk of the twelfth century so lingers in the memory; like Anselm of Bec, he escapes from his age, though most typical of it, and speaks directly to us, as, in fuller measure, Augustine and Teresa speak, of his restless search for One to whom he might give the full strength of his love. As we read, a corner of the veil that hides the past from us seems to lift, and we catch a momentary glimpse of Rievaulx in its first eagerness—a glimpse that reveals something unexpected, at once most real and yet most alien to our habits of thought.

A true Cistercian in his simplicity and austerity, Ailred is also a true disciple of Bernard in the warmth of sentiment which makes more than one of his pages a counterpart of the Sermons on the Canticle. He resembles Bernard, also, in his ability to administer and organize, and in the attractive power of his mind, which made of him the counsellor and confidant of many in high places far from Rievaulx. Like Bernard, too, he had a wide correspondence, and preached and wrote in the meditative, discursive manner that was so soon to give way to the new discipline of the schools. But Ailred cannot be wholly described in terms of Bernard. He lacks altogether the triumphant and compelling force, as also the consuming zeal, of the abbot of Clairvaux; he has, on the other hand, something altogether his own, a delicacy, an intuition which, from being a gift of mind alone, gradually came to be a reflection of the whole spirit, and which makes of his later years of rule at Rievaulx an episode altogether *sui generis* in English monastic life. It is not easy to think of another in that age—unless it be Abelard—who so arouses and baffles all our endeavours to comprehend what comes so near to us and yet remains so far away.

Ailred was by birth completely English, with an ancestry that gave him connections with the Church stretching far back into the Northumbrian past (for his father was 'hereditary' priest of Hexham), and with the landed families between Hexham and Durham. Though he was not trained in the schools as were his contemporaries who crossed to France, he had clearly been well taught, probably at Hexham, by one who was familiar with the new humanism, and when still in the impressionable years of late boyhood he became one of the court circle of the Scottish king and ultimately held the post of steward or seneschal. At that period, the rivalry between the Scottish and English had little of the racial significance it afterwards came to acquire. The kings of Scotland were of the blood royal of pre-Conquest England, and were in a sense the legitimate sovereigns of Englishmen; David had an earldom in the south, and was often at the court of Henry I; the district between the Humber and the Cheviot was still debatable ground. If the Scottish king claimed sovereignty over counties soon to be wholly English, the archbishop of York, on his side, claimed metropolitan rights far north of the

Tweed, and more than one Englishman had tried his fortune in a Scottish see. Ailred had been brought up with David's son, Henry, and there was, therefore, nothing unusual in his presence at the Scottish court, as there was nothing strange in the Scottish king's English stepson, Waldef, entering a religious house in Yorkshire. The author of Ailred's *Life*, and Jocelin of Furness who composed the *Life* of Waldef, dwell naturally upon the temptations of court life. These were doubtless considerable, but the Scottish court had during the past fifty years been something of a nursery of saints. The exquisite St Margaret, King David's mother, herself a grand-niece of the Confessor, had in her husband, Malcolm, and still more in her son, David, and daughter, Matilda of England, a family not unworthy of her. In the next generation David's second wife, besides bringing him a stepson later to be venerated as St Waldef, brought also traditions of the boy's grandfather, the Earl Waltheof whom nationalist sentiment had invested with the halo of martyrdom. In addition to its tradition of sanctity, the Scottish royal house was distinguished by personal courage and administrative ability of a high order, so that the atmosphere, even if there was little culture in it, must have been morally bracing to a degree for a generous and receptive nature. Certainly Ailred, impressionable from a child, became deeply attached to David, and his biographer tells us that the king intended him for the highest ecclesiastical preferment in his dominions. This, however, was not to be. Already, as a young man of about twenty, he must have been stirred by the action of his friend Waldef, the king's stepson and brother of Simon, earl of Northumberland, who about 1130 became an Augustinian canon at Nostell, then under the rule of Aldulf. Within a few years the distinguished young canon became prior of Kirkham, a house founded by Walter Espec only a few miles from the still desert valley of the Rye, and there

Ailred was soon to find his friend again, and his own heart's home.

Gentleness, radiance of affection and wide sympathy are not the qualities which most would associate with the early Cistercians, but they are assuredly the outstanding natural characteristics of Ailred. As a child and boy, his whole life had been given to his friends:

When I was still a boy at school, the friendship of those around me was my greatest joy, and in all the occupations and dangers of those years I gave myself wholly up to my affection for my friends, so that to love and to be loved seemed the most delightful thing in the world, and nothing else seemed of any profit at all.[1]

Cicero's *De Amicitia* was put into his hands as a text-book. He read it eagerly, and felt regret that his own friendships seemed to fall so far short of the grave and measured standards required by the philosopher. As a boy and young man at David's court his heart still gave itself readily, perhaps all the more readily because his friends had the glamour of a higher birth than his own. His years in Scotland were sour-sweet days. They gave him a loving admiration for his patron David which never faded from his mind, and a deep friendship for David's son, Henry—a friendship which had, indeed, roots still deeper in the past—and his stepson, Waldef, but they were years of a long struggle which he records in the cadences, and almost in the phrases, of the most familiar pages of Augustine. Here, again, besides an anguish the nature of which we can but surmise, it was his heart that kept him from his heart's true rest:

The ties of that life among friends held me, and above all the knot of one friendship, dear to me above all the delights of the life that then

[1] Ailred's *amari et amare* is of course an echo of Augustine's description of his early life in *Confessions*, II, 2: 'Et quid erat, quod me delectabat, nisi amare et amari?'

37

was mine.... Those about me, seeing what I possessed, but ignorant what was passing within me, said: How well it is with him! They little knew how ill it was with me within, where alone true joy can be.

The contest was so bitter that for a time death seemed to him the only solution that might rid him of his burden. Whether the break with the past in his soul was accomplished before his arrival at Rievaulx, he does not tell us, but the manner of that homecoming is related by his biographer. Ailred was sent south, about 1134, on a mission from King David to Archbishop Thurstan. He heard from a friend, probably Waldef, of the white monks who had arrived two years before at Rievaulx, though it can scarcely have been the first time he had heard of those whom King David had helped. Anxious to visit them, he was taken by his friend to Helmsley, where they stayed the night with Walter Espec and passed the next day at the new monastery. After another night with Espec, Ailred was setting out for Scotland when, riding along the ridge of the hill above Rievaulx, he could no longer resist the Spirit. Again he presented himself at the door, and this time he had come to remain.

In his early days at Rievaulx he was still most sensitive to the affectionate influence of those about him. Among them was the monk Simon, younger than himself, who died still young shortly before Ailred wrote the *Speculum Charitatis* eight years later, and whom he laments in pages which, though they owe something to Bernard's lament on his brother composed some three years previously, and still more to those in which Augustine mourned Nebridius and Monica, are no less a revelation of his own deep emotion:

I remember (he writes) how often, when my eyes were straying hither and thither, the mere sight of him so filled me with shame that, returning suddenly to myself, I sternly repressed my lightness of mind, and recollecting myself, began to think of something of more profit.

The rule of our life forbade us to talk together, but his countenance, his gait, his very silence spoke to me.

Almost twenty years later, the memory of Simon was still fresh; for Ailred was faithful in his love:

I recall two friends (he says) who although they may have passed from this life yet live to me and always will live. The first I took as my friend when still young at the beginning of my religious life; our tastes, our characters were something similar.... He was snatched from me at the very beginning of our friendship, when he had been chosen, but not fully proved....

Ailred's years in the court circle of King David had doubt-less given a distinction to his bearing, and we know him to have been, as a young man, unusually handsome. Abbot William soon singled out the young monk whose past history and qualities of mind, added to his growing holiness, must have distinguished him to any discerning observer, and in 1142 we find him sent as the abbot's representative to Rome in the matter of the York election. It can scarcely be doubted that he met Bernard as he passed through France, and that it was at this meeting that the abbot of Clairvaux first made the request that Ailred should write on Charity—a request which he repeated shortly with such compelling force. His letter found Ailred novice master at Rievaulx, and it was answered by the *Speculum Charitatis* written, as his biographer tells us, in the *probatorium*. A year later he was appointed abbot of the new foundation of Revesby in Lincolnshire.

Ailred became abbot of Rievaulx in 1147, when he was some thirty-seven years of age, and held the office till he died, a man whom long illness had made prematurely old in body, in the first days of 1167. The period of his rule, a little more than nineteen years long, was one of very great prosperity for the house in things material and spiritual, and one in which

Ailred's great and in many ways unique gifts of mind and soul came to full maturity.

The material growth of Rievaulx can be traced in the record of benefactions provided by its cartulary and the reconstructions that have been made of the plan of its early buildings, but the personal direction of Ailred effected its most striking work in the building up of the family of the house. He was, his biographer tells us, 'of extreme delicacy of feeling, condescending to the weakness of all, nor did he think that any who besought him for charity's sake should be saddened'. Hence:

In receiving those who desired to come to religion he made as though he would have gone further,[1] that the prayers of the brethren might press him, as one unwilling, to consent; hence it came about that many were received of whom he had no real knowledge, for he often left it to the judgment of the community to receive whom they would.

A result of this condescension was an enormous increase of the numbers at Rievaulx. If we may receive as definite Ailred's own figures and those of Walter Daniel, the community which in 1132 may have numbered only twenty-five had risen to three hundred by 1142 and to six hundred and fifty by 1165.

Ailred's biographer, in a vivid phrase, describes the crowded church on feast days, when the majority of the *conversi* would be back from the granges, as packed with monks as closely as a hive with bees; so close that they cannot stir, and resembling crowded choirs of angels as pictured by devout fancy. The coming of such large numbers to Rievaulx was not merely the response of the north to the call of Cîteaux, still less was it due to a good-natured *laissez-faire* on the part of the abbot; it was Ailred's explicit desire and invitation. He never tired of

[1] The reference is to Luke xxiv. 28–9: 'He made as though he would have gone further. But they constrained him, saying: Abide with us, etc.'

repeating that the supreme and singular glory of Rievaulx was
that it had learnt, beyond all other houses, to bear with the
weak and to have compassion on those in need:

All (he said), strong and weak alike, should find in Rievaulx a haven
of peace, a spacious and calm home...of it should be said: Thither
the tribes go up, the tribes of the Lord, unto the testimony of Israel,
to give thanks unto the name of the Lord. Yea, tribes of the strong
and of the weak. For that cannot be called a house of religion which
spurns the weak, since: Thine eyes have seen mine imperfection and
in thy book are all written.

And so there flocked to Ailred men of every type from near
and far:

Was there ever (asks Walter Daniel) anyone weak in body or
character expelled from that house unless his evil ways gave offence
to the whole community or ruined his own hope of salvation? Hence
there came to Rievaulx from foreign nations and distant lands a stream
of monks who needed brotherly mercy and true compassion, and
there they found the peace and sanctity without which no man can
see God. Yea, those who were restless in the world and to whom no
religious house gave entry, coming to Rievaulx the mother of mercy
and finding the gates wide open, freely entered therein.

Clearly for Ailred the Cistercian way of life was no garden
enclosed, in which only rare and pure souls would find green
pasture, but rather something in its way as catholic as the
Church, a home for souls of every kind who should find each
the help most suited to him. And it must not be forgotten
that three out of every four who came were simple, unlettered,
stolid labourers, come to swell the ranks of an army of *conversi*.
The dangers accompanying such a policy as Ailred's are
obvious, and must have been so to his own clear mind. But
the influence of such a man as he was can scarcely be over-
estimated, and all the evidence that exists points to the maintenance at Rievaulx of a sustained fervour for many decades
after his death. Ailred's condescension was not weakness or

compromise; the strict rule of Cîteaux was honoured, and the latter years of the abbot's life, when his physical suffering was all but unceasing, must have made it abundantly clear that the way of mercy was not the way of delicate living.

More than two-thirds of the family of Rievaulx were made up of the *conversi*, and it is certain that of the choir monks many, no doubt the majority, were men of no refinement or intellectual gifts. Yet all the sources reveal the existence, alike at Rievaulx and the other houses of Ailred's family, of a numerous class of monks who had passed through the new humanist discipline of the schools and retained, even within the framework of the Cistercian life of labour, silence and simplicity, a warm eagerness of mind and heart which few who visit the ruins of Rievaulx would associate with its walls. It was with these that Ailred's relations were at once most characteristic and most individual. Hard though it be to fill in the details of the picture, the main outlines are given us, clear beyond the possibility of misconception, by Gilbert of Holland, Walter Daniel and Ailred himself. We see him, the Cistercian abbot, the centre of a group of listeners and interlocutors, engaged in one of those discussions, half Platonic, half scholastic in character, which in one form or another absorbed for more than two centuries the interests and energies of so many in Western Europe. With Ailred, especially in his later years, the aim was primarily spiritual, not intellectual, but the young monks who surrounded him had, like himself, steeped themselves in Cicero and followed the young Augustine; they had even given themselves to a newer spirit, that of the Arthurian romance; they had much to learn and to leave before they could follow Ailred with the fourth gospel to the Cross. We can watch him treating with one such, the young monk Gratian, to whom two of the three dialogues *De Spirituali Amicitia* are principally addressed, and who is introduced to us in words put by Ailred in the mouth of no other than Walter Daniel as: 'One whom I might fitly call friendship's child; for his whole occupation is to love and to be loved.'

Ailred had learnt much since the days at David's court. He now defines friendship with his eyes upon the later chapters of St John's gospel: All things which I have heard of my Father, I make known unto you; and: You are my friends if you do what I command you.

By these words (he continues), as St Ambrose says, he gave us a way of friendship to follow, that we should do the will of our friend, that we should lay bare the secrets of our heart to our friend, and know his in return....A friend hides nothing. If he be a true friend, he pours out his soul, as the Lord Jesus poured forth the mysteries of the Father. Thus Ambrose. But how many do we not love, to whom it is unwise to open our soul and pour forth all that is within! Either their age or their understanding is unable to bear it.

To this Walter Daniel replies:

This friendship is so sublime and perfect that I dare not aspire to it. Gratian here and I are content with that described by your favourite Augustine[1]—to talk together, to laugh together, to do each other services, to read together, to study together, to share things trifling and serious; sometimes to disagree, but without passion, as a man may do with himself, and by such disagreement to season the number-less judgments which we share together; to teach and learn the one from the other, to feel the want of our friends when absent, and welcome their coming with joy. Such signs of heart-felt affection as these, translating themselves upon the countenance, or in the speech and eyes of those who love each other, and in a thousand affectionate gestures, are like tinder to set hearts on fire, and to make of many one mind and heart. This it is that we think to be lovable in our friends, so that our conscience seems guilty, if we do not return another's love, whether he or we first gave it.

[1] The reference is to *Confessions*, IV, 8.

To which Ailred:

This is the friendship of the flesh and above all of the young, as were once the writer of these words and the friend of whom he spoke. Yet, saving trifles and deceits, if nothing evil enters in, it may be tolerated in hopes of more abundant grace to come, and as the foundation of a more holy friendship. As one grows in the religious life, and in spiritual discipline, together with the gravity of maturer years and the enlightenment of spiritual understanding, such friendships pass easily into higher regions, as the affections become purified. For we said yesterday that it was easy to pass from man's friendship to God's, by reason of the resemblance between them.

This passage has been quoted at length, as showing Ailred at his most characteristic. In its outspoken humanism and serene optimism it recalls the atmosphere of the Academy or of Tusculum, and indeed the two chief treatises of Ailred are documents not yet perhaps sufficiently familiar to historians of the culture and religious sentiment of the times. The later dialogue, from which the quotations have been taken, ends with a long account of two of Ailred's own friendships.

I recall two friends (he says) who, 'although they have passed from this life yet live to me and always will live. The first I took as my friend when still young. [This, as we have seen, was the monk Simon.] The other[1] was chosen by me when he was still a boy; I tested him in many, many ways, and when I was now growing old I took him into my most intimate friendship. The first I chose as friend and companion in the joys of the cloister and the delights of the spirit which I was then tasting for the first time; I had no burden of the care of souls upon me yet, and no anxiety over temporal things. I asked nothing, I bestowed nothing, but affection, and the loving judgment which affection gave. The other I took, when he was still young, to a share in my solicitudes, and had him as my helper in this work of mine. So far as my memory serves to judge these two friendships, I would say that the former rested more on affection, the latter on reason, though in the latter there was affection too, and the former

---

[1] The second friend, who came from abroad and was ultimately subprior, cannot be identified.

was not without reason. But while the one friend, who was taken from me in the very beginnings of our friendship, could be chosen, as I have said, but not tested, the other was spared to me from boyhood to middle age and loved by me, and passed with me through all the stages of friendship.

And Ailred, after describing their life together, ends:

And thus, beseeching Christ on behalf of one's friend, and for the friend's sake desiring to be heard by Christ, the attention and affection are all directed to the friend; but suddenly and unawares love changes its object, and being so near touches the sweetness of Christ and begins to taste and feel how sweet he is. Thus rising from that holy love which reaches the friend to that which reaches Christ, he will joyfully pluck the rich spiritual fruit of friendship...and this friendship, to which few are admitted, will be poured out upon all and returned by all to God, when God shall be all in all.

The writer of these lines was not a philosopher, writing at ease on his terrace, untroubled by the hard realities of life, nor even an Augustine among his pupils in peaceful, sunny Cassiciacum, but an infirm, tireless abbot, the ruler of a vast household, the counsellor of bishops and kings, who snatched time, between his solitary prayer and the visits of those who needed his help, to add a few sentences to the roll in his bare and comfortless cell. Besides the responsibility for all things material and spiritual at Rievaulx, Ailred had no rest from the obligation of long and regularly recurring journeys. The framers of the *Carta Caritatis*, writing for a small group of houses situated in a single region of one country, little realized when they wrote what a ceaseless labour of journeying to and fro was to be the lot of the abbots of mother-houses in the near future. By their regulations, increased by later statute, every Cistercian abbot had to visit every year both Cîteaux, for the general chapter in September, and the abbey of which his own was a filiation. He had also to perform the regular yearly visitation of all the daughter-houses of his own home. Thus

Ailred, in the course of each year, had the obligation of visiting Cîteaux, Clairvaux, Woburn, Revesby, Rufford, Melrose and Dundrennan, and though no doubt dispensations or sheer impossibility relieved him from time to time of some of these visits, there is evidence from a number of sources that none of his charges was neglected, and that he was continually on the road. Clairvaux was doubtless taken on the way to or from Cîteaux, and the three English houses could be visited on the same journey with little waste of time, but it was a long circuit to Melrose and Galloway (there is evidence that Ailred made this journey in the early spring), and the two absences must have accounted for some three or four months of a year.

These regular appearances of such a distinguished man as Ailred, the intimate friend of the king of Scotland, at the centres of life along the great roads, must have served as an incitement to many to make use of his counsel or his eloquence, and he became more and more a public figure, one of the most considerable in the north of England. David of Scotland was his friend, and in England, among others, Robert, earl of Leicester, the justiciar, and Gilbert Foliot, the active bishop of Hereford and London. He had addressed a work to Henry II before 1154 and the acquaintance ripened in after years; we are told that his advice had the greatest influence over the king in determining him to support Alexander III against the antipope Octavian in 1159. His presence as arbitrator or adviser was desired by religious superiors and communities of every order, and he came to be sought after as a preacher for great occasions. As early as 1147 he arbitrated on a question of the prior of Durham's precedence; in 1151 he gave judgment in the dispute between Savigny and Furness for jurisdiction over Byland; in 1155 he preached at Hexham on the occasion of a solemn translation of relics; in 1163 he was present at the council at Westminster that decided the question of exemption between St Albans and the bishop of Lincoln, and in the same year he preached at the translation of the relics of Edward the Confessor, recently canonized; in 1164 he attested an important agreement between the orders of Cîteaux and Sempringham.

No doubt his good offices were often solicited also by individuals. A casual reference shows him visiting, in company with a young monk from the neighbouring monastery of Durham, the celebrated Godric of Finchale, and he himself tells us how he was called in by Gilbert of Sempringham to advise in the case of the strange happenings at Watton.

Along with these external activities went a steady output of writing. If in 1142 it had required the direct and reiterated command of Bernard to make him break silence, in later life he gave himself more readily to composition of all kinds, and even became something of a historian laureate. His first venture in this field would seem to have been his account of the Battle of the Standard; it was followed by his *Genealogy of the Kings of England*, written in 1152–3, which was addressed to the future Henry II when Duke of Normandy and celebrated the union of the Norman and old English royal lines; by a patriotic account of the saints of Hexham a year or two later; and by a life, destined to become standard, of Edward the Confessor composed *c.* 1163. In another category are the monastic conferences and the sermons on Isaiah, which belong to the same years, together with the more characteristic and elaborate dialogues on Spiritual Friendship and the Soul, the latter of which was unfinished at his death; nor did he refuse a request such as that of his sister, from her anchor-hold, for a rule of life. Literary activities of a theological or devotional nature, though a departure from the original scheme of Cîteaux, could find ample precedent in the life of Bernard, but the historical treatises of Ailred came *de son cru*, as the work of a northerner whose earliest memories were of traditions of Bede. They show, as do Ailred's discussions with a circle of his monks, that the *Carta Caritatis* and the Cistercian statutes, though in appearance so devoid of elasticity, were in practice capable of receiving new wine without being broken.

Besides these formal compositions Ailred began, at about the time of his first literary venture in 1143, to open a correspondence which in time came to count among its recipients the pope, the kings of France, England and Scotland, almost all the bishops, and magnates such as the earl of Leicester. Walter Daniel assures us, and we may believe him, that in these letters Ailred's spirit left its most living memorial; most unfortunately they have all disappeared, save for one or two epistles prefatory to his works.

Ailred was not a deep speculative or mystical theologian; he was not conversant with the dialectic that had developed so speedily in Europe during his lifetime, and he lacked Bernard's gift of grasping and expounding in magisterial manner a question of moral or spiritual importance. He had, indeed, an extremely sympathetic and alert mind, and the most superficial examination of his writings finds in them reflections of the thought of the time—in the earlier treatises of the Cistercian controversies and Bernard's writings, in the later of the topics discussed by Hugh and Richard of St Victor—but they are reflections and no more; Ailred was not of the schools and did not probe deeply into the mysteries of the faith. His unique position as a writer—wholly unique in England, and without exact parallel abroad—is due in part to the limpid sincerity with which he laid bare, in his wish to help others, the growth and progress of his own mind and heart from the human to the divine, and in part to the candid humanism of his most characteristic pages.

The demands which his various duties and employments

made upon the mental and physical energies of the abbot of Rievaulx would have taxed to the uttermost the strength of one in perfect health. Ailred, during the last ten years of his life, was, like his master at Clairvaux, constantly ill and subject to recurring visitations of pain which left him prostrate and unable to stir. To a chronic disease which resembled gout or rheumatic fever in that it rendered him incapable of motion and acutely sensitive to the slightest touch, were added attacks of the stone in which he could do nothing but lie on a piece of matting by the fire in the infirmary, frail and twisted as a crumpled sheet of parchment. During all these ten years he made use of a dispensation obtained from general chapter which permitted him to live in the infirmary and yet at the same time, whenever possible, travel about his lands and granges and take full part in all community duties. Walter Daniel gives a vivid description of the shed which he caused to be constructed for himself alongside of the common infirmary, with two divisions. In one of these was his pallet, in the other his oratory; in the former he received his sons, who came to him in their numbers, sitting or standing about the room or on his very bed 'as little children might on that of their mother'; in the other he wrote his letters and treatises, and spent many of the night hours in prayer. During the last four years of his life his austerities and prayers increased with his infirmities, and he ceased to care for the advice of physicians; he often returned from Mass so exhausted that he lay as one dead for an hour, yet he never failed to carry out effectively the administration of his house.

The last phase of his illness came upon him on Christmas Eve, 1166. A few days later he took a formal farewell of the community round his bed, and gave to them the small objects that had been so long and constantly used in his hours of vigil —a glossed psalter, Augustine's *Confessions*, a text of St John

49

and Henry Murdac's crucifix. His biographer more than once remarks on the charm which never left him, and on the love of his sons which brought them in crowds—even to the number of a hundred—to his bedside. He adds, in a paragraph of singular beauty:

For myself, I must confess that while I felt a great awe as I stood by his bed during those days, yet I felt also a joy greater than the awe. For we heard him saying continually: 'Hasten, hasten,' and he often urged his request with the name of Christ, which he spoke in English, because Christ's name in that tongue is of only one syllable, and is easier to pronounce and more pleasant to hear. He kept saying, then, to give his very words: 'Hasten, for Crist luve.' And when I said to him: 'What is it, father?' he lifted his hands towards heaven and his eyes, shining like fire, to the crucifix over against him, and said: 'Suffer me to depart as soon as may be to Him, the king of glory, whom I see before me. Why do you delay? What are you about? What do you wait for? Hasten, for Christ's love, hasten.' I say to all who shall read this page that never in all my life have I been so moved as when hearing those words so often repeated, uttered in a way that struck such awe, by such a man at such a moment, by a man of such holiness at the hour of his death. And these words were ever upon his lips for the space of three days.

On the day before his death, 11 January 1167, Richard, abbot of Fountains, Roger, abbot of Byland, and almost all his choir monks, together with some *conversi*, were about him. He could not speak, but followed with his heart the Passion as it was read to him. Walter Daniel, who was holding the dying abbot's head in his hands, whispered to him, so low that no one could hear: 'Father, look upon the crucifix; let your eyes be where your heart is.' Ailred, who had not spoken for two days, at once opened his eyes, and gazing at the figure on the cross said: 'Thou art my Lord and my God, thou art my refuge and my salvation, thou art my glory and my hope for ever. Into thy hands I commit my spirit.' He did not speak again.

VII

HENRY OF WINCHESTER

Henry of Blois (? 1101–71), brother of King Stephen, was a young monk at Cluny when invited by his uncle, King Henry I, to come to England as abbot of Glastonbury in 1126. In 1129 he was appointed bishop of Winchester, and for the rest of his life continued to control the wealthiest see and the wealthiest abbey of the country. When his brother became king of England in 1132 he took a leading and not always an edifying part in the intrigues, and later in the warfare, of Stephen's reign; for some years he was the greatest power in the ecclesiastical life of the country. When Henry II became king in 1154 he fell out of favour and was for a time in exile, returning to live in semi-retirement. He sympathized with the cause of Archbishop Thomas Becket without actively supporting him. He founded at Winchester the Hospital of St Cross, which still exists.

HENRY OF BLOIS, younger brother of King Stephen, and thus nephew of Henry I and cousin of Henry II, was in many ways a very remarkable man. As a king-maker he has only one rival in English history, the celebrated Earl of Warwick, as a bishop he has been hailed by that eminent scholar, Edmund Bishop, as the greatest uncanonized English prelate of his century, and as a supremely able financier and administrator he manifested in one theatre after another the genius of a Woolton or a Keynes, while as a connoisseur and collector of antiques he was without a rival in his age. Appointed by a royal act of power to the abbey of Glastonbury in his twenties, and to the wealthy bishopric of Winchester when he was thirty, he was for some eight years (1135–43), during four of which he was papal legate with precedence over the archbishop of Canterbury, unquestionably the most powerful agency in England both in secular and in ecclesiastical politics, which indeed became inextricably mingled in his hands. While holding high Gregorian views as to the centralization of the Church and the paramountcy of the spiritual power, he nevertheless used every opportunity and all his influence to promote relatives and protégés to bishoprics and abbacies. For himself he undoubtedly desired the see of Canterbury, to which indeed he was formally elected on the death of William of Corbeil in 1136. For a translation, however, papal permission was traditionally a *sine qua non*, and Henry, in addition to his political foes, had powerful religious adversaries in the persons of St Bernard and other leading Cistercians. The abbot of Clairvaux in particular was a tireless agitator against one who by his political intrigues, his wealth, his martial exploits, his pluralism and his nepotism outraged, in the eyes of the reformers, not only the monastic but the Christian conscience of the whole of Europe, and the 'old wizard of Winchester' or, still more forcibly, the 'whore of Winchester', figures in more than one of the saint's most lively letters. Henry's election to Canterbury, therefore, was never confirmed.

Consoled by a legation which set him above the new archbishop, Theobald, during several years he administered two dioceses besides his own see and the abbey of Glastonbury; not content with this, he conceived the remarkable project of erecting Winchester into a metropolitan see with six suffragans. This scheme, too, foundered on curial intrigue or papal prudence, but Henry remained the most powerful ecclesiastic in the country till the death of Stephen, despite several maladroit political moves and changes of front. Although he had favoured the young Henry and assisted him in his first days, the bishop of Winchester, an intolerably overmighty subject with a group of private castles, was an anachronism in the new world of 1154, and having transferred the bulk of his

PLATE III

HENRY OF BLOIS

PLATE IV

ST FRANCIS OF ASSISI

funds abroad he followed them without asking for licence, and spent some years in reorganizing the finances and economics of Cluny, the monastic home of his few years in the cloister. He returned to England for good in time to consecrate, as *doyen* of the hierarchy, the new archbishop of Canterbury in 1162, and thenceforward was deeply concerned in all the phases of the controversy. Although Thomas had in the past been chiefly instrumental in obtaining the legateship for Theobald in opposition to the bishop of Winchester, and more recently as chancellor must have lent a hand in demolishing Henry's castles, the bishop bore no malice. Indeed, for all the adventures and intrigues and extravagances and ambitions of his middle life, which at first glance seem to anticipate the worst characteristics of a Beaufort or a Wolsey, Henry had remained not only blameless in his private life, but also unsoured, unhardened and undefiled.

All his contemporaries agree that in this last period of his life his character had greatly changed; perhaps it would be more true to say that the deepest potentialities of his personality, long undeveloped beneath the turmoil of ambitious and worldly activities, now had freedom to spring into life and view. Leaving intrigues and taunts to others, he became to all a venerable and beloved elder statesman, retiring further and further from his ambitions and even from his riches as he drew nearer to death. Consequently, his direct part in the great controversy was not large—one who had known him twenty years before could hardly have imagined him swept along so passively on the stream of events. Partly, no doubt, this was due to age, partly to a changed spiritual outlook, and partly to deliberate policy, but the deepest reason of all was perhaps a trait of character. Henry of Blois, though a very able, a curiously amiable, and in some respects even an admirable man, was not, either as a man of action or as a man of thought, absolutely great. Though more resolute and more practical than his brother, he had something of Stephen's inconsequence. Neither his political nor his ecclesiastical activities were informed by far-sighted policies or ideals, or even by firm consistency; they were all intensely personal and opportunist. Consequently, in his last and most attractive phase the great issue between king and archbishop made no challenge to him for a last and best fight. He passes through the pages of the *Materials for the History of Thomas Becket* if not precisely as a ghost, a *revenant*, yet as something of a survival, as it might be a dowager with the light of a falling day about her. His wealth, his influence, his venerable age, his legendary past, his amiable and devout present, all combined to make him a personality to be reckoned with by all parties.

We are in one respect at a disadvantage in judging him. While his figure meets us at every turn for half a century, and while evidences and monuments of his activity are numberless, no collection of his letters has been preserved. Letters—a numerous and varied collection of letters—are the best of all mirrors of a man's character and mind and motives, whether he be a Cicero or a Bernard. We have only to recollect how much precious light is thrown upon Henry's contemporaries—Bernard himself, Peter of Cluny, Gilbert Foliot—by their correspondence to realize what such a collection would tell us of the bishop of Winchester. Failing this, we can but judge him by his actions, such as we know of them, and through his contemporaries.

Henry of Blois, though not precisely a complex character—for throughout all his activities there is the same stamp of energy and directness of purpose—was certainly a man of many-sided qualities. The commander who erected half a dozen fortresses in his diocese and burnt out his episcopal city, together with a great monastery and nunnery, was also the man who rebuilt Glastonbury on a grand scale, who re-established Cluny, who founded the hospital of St Cross, and who decorated his cathedral with the most precious and varied works of art, from the fonts which still remain to illuminations and enamels and masterpieces of the goldsmith's art which have almost entirely disappeared. The patron of William of Malmesbury in the reign of Henry I and of Gerald of Wales in that of Henry II was also the friend of St William of York, of St Gilbert of Sempringham, of St Thomas of Canterbury, and—though not without periods of coolness—of Peter the Venerable; while to St Bernard and Eugenius III he was the old enemy, the seducer.

He was undoubtedly a man of extraordinary capacity for administration and organization. Not once only, but in at least four different theatres—at Glastonbury, at Winchester, both in the affairs of St Swithun's and in the administration of the diocese, and at Cluny in 1156–7—did he rescue and restore to order the affairs of great corporations. At Cluny, moreover, when an exile and sixty years of age, he not only took the complex machinery of the whole economic administration into his hands, and produced a new scheme of 'rationalization', but supported the entire community for a year out of his private resources. In all these undertakings we see the same thorough methods, the same grasp of detail and of the whole behind the parts, and it is natural to see a kinship of mind between Henry of Winchester and those leaders of great industrial concerns who in our own day have been called at a moment of crisis from one department of industry or finance to another, and from private to national spheres of activity. Perhaps the greatest testimony to his supreme ability is the regard which the monks of Glastonbury always cherished for him. Great indeed must have been the practical benefits of his government which could outweigh the numberless disadvantages of having as abbot for forty years a foreigner and an absentee. Yet later generations at Glastonbury agree with William of Malmesbury in looking upon Henry's abbacy as a time of peace and prosperity. To the monks of St Swithun's and of Cluny, likewise, he appeared and remained a mercy and a benediction.

As an ecclesiastical statesman, he left his mark on England chiefly by throwing the door wide open to intercourse and appeals from this country to the Curia, but in the evolution of ideas he is perhaps still more significant as being a Cluniac who held the full Gregorian conception of church government, but treated it as a political programme rather than as a moral ideal, and was therefore ready to concede and barter, just as he was ready to employ material arms in its execution or use it for personal aggrandizement. In all this, he stood at the opposite extreme, among the statesmen of the Church, to the school of reform that drew inspiration from Clairvaux. As to his wealth and magnificence, all witnesses at all periods of his public life are agreed. To his princely buildings at Glastonbury, at Winchester and at Cluny, and his truly regal gifts to his English churches, must be added his own magnificent establishments, with their statues, their jewels, their gardens and their menageries. He was the first amateur of art of his age, and his taste extended even to the remains of classical antiquity. Eloquent, persuasive, sagacious, and for all his drastic energy not without diplomatic tact and finesse, he was above all a man of the firmest purpose where his interests were engaged.[1] Yet for all his strength, in which he far surpassed his brother, he had at all times, but especially in

[1] A striking example of this was seen when his request for the erection of Winchester into a separate ecclesiastical province was refused by the pope. Henry proceeded to ask for exemption for his diocese from Theobald's jurisdiction, and when this was refused he asked for a personal exemption.

his later years, a full measure of that amiability which all remarked in Stephen; it is noteworthy, and to the credit of all the three men concerned, that he never allowed his public quarrel with Theobald to embitter their personal relations, and that the cloud that passed over his friendship with Peter of Cluny was but temporary.

Such were some of Henry's admirable qualities; he had others which suited less with his office and his profession. Without question he was personally ambitious; he desired power and independence not principally for some higher end, but for themselves. From the moment that he eagerly entered the arena of secular politics till the death of Stephen he was in a false position from which no amount of sagacity or moderation could extricate him. The familiar and bitter phrase of Henry of Huntingdon was at bottom true, and nothing could redeem the combination of elements essentially hostile one to another.[1] Henry's acts of ruthlessness and tergiversation, so unlike his later and truer self, were indeed due to his position, but they were also due to his own choice. Even less susceptible of justification were his high-handed and selfish actions in the purely religious sphere. Strangely enough, no contemporary was found to blame explicitly his retention of Glastonbury during his forty years of episcopal life, but whatever excuses he may have found for himself from reasons of expediency such a practice was uncanonical, contrary to all monastic principle, and a precedent for the worst abuses. Similarly, his persistent and often successful efforts to obtain bishoprics and abbacies for his relatives and supporters, and his little less than outrageous schemes, based purely on personal motives, for changing the whole framework of the English hierarchy, betray an outlook very different from that of one who considers only the spiritual end of a spiritual office. It was this

---

[1] He called the bishop 'a new kind of monster, a monk-soldier'.

subordination of the spiritual to a policy of alliance and personal influence that drew upon Henry the vehement disapproval of Bernard, the Cistercians of the north and Eugenius III who, it must be remembered, knew him only in his years of ambition. We do not, indeed, know the cause of the coolness which existed between him and even Peter the Venerable during some years of this period, but it is not unnatural to suppose that the abbot of Cluny, though more tolerant by nature than the abbot of Clairvaux, was out of sympathy with much in Henry's way of acting. This estrangement passed wholly, the great Cistercians died long before the bishop of Winchester, and he himself mingled in the events of the next generation with a character deepened and softened by age. Yet though the part he played was of great and often of decisive importance, Henry of Winchester, we feel, fell short of absolute greatness, both as an ecclesiastical statesman and as a diocesan bishop. He was neither a Lanfranc nor a Grosseteste. And the reason behind such a judgment would seem to be that he lacked, during the years of his greatest power, both the intellectual greatness needed for conceiving a policy and its means of execution, and the moral greatness essential in one who is to concentrate on a single aim devoid of personal interest. When, in his last years, he gave himself more fully to his spiritual duties and to the things of God, it was not by exercising his unusual gifts of administration nor by satisfying his exquisite artistic taste, but rather by his withdrawal from external activities, that he regained something of his first vocation and found his true peace.

VIII

GILBERT FOLIOT

Gilbert Foliot (? 1110–87) entered the abbey of Cluny after a training in the schools; he rose rapidly and became abbot of Gloucester in 1139, was appointed bishop of Hereford by Pope Eugenius III, and translated to London in 1163. Before the election of Becket to Canterbury he was regarded as the spiritual leader of the bishops; subsequently he became the archbishop's most bitter opponent.

GILBERT FOLIOT came of a distinguished Anglo-Norman family which gave other sons to high ecclesiastical office. Originally a monk at Cluny, he was, when still a very young man, appointed prior, and subsequently prior of Abbeville. In 1139 at the motion of his relative Milo, earl of Hereford, and no doubt with the approval of Henry of Blois, he was made abbot of Gloucester, a flourishing house whence his brother had recently been taken to become abbot of Evesham. From this date till his death almost fifty years later we can follow his external activities in his voluminous correspondence.

As abbot of Gloucester his abilities speedily drew the attention of his contemporaries; we can watch him in his letters taking an increasing share in political and ecclesiastical affairs. While maintaining Gloucester at the high level of observance inherited from Serlo he took an interest in other houses, especially Cerne in Dorset, where he consistently both in public and private supported the party of reform under Bernard, a monk of his own abbey. In 1148 he was appointed bishop of Hereford directly by the pope, Eugenius III, to whom he was known as a supporter of the Empress, a strongly Gregorian ecclesiastic, and an upright man. It is noteworthy that he endeavoured, but without success, to retain the abbey of Gloucester when bishop. During his years at Hereford his influence continued to grow steadily; at the death of Theobald he was without question the most outstanding member of the hierarchy now that Henry of Winchester was settling to his quiet old age; he was the new king's spiritual adviser, and it was freely said that he hoped for the primatial see to which, in the event, Thomas Becket was appointed. If this were so, as it may well have been, he must have received some satisfaction when he was translated, at Becket's recommendation, to the important see of London. Friendly relations, however, between the two prelates, whatever their original sincerity, did not long endure. As is well known, Foliot was the leader of the party among the bishops which was opposed to the primate's sudden reversal of policy and subsequent refusal to compromise; in a moment of passion he told Becket that a fool he was and a fool he always had been, and in a long letter to the exiled archbishop in which the measured sentences, like points of steel, are driven home by the intense feeling of the writer, he travelled over the whole dispute. We are not here concerned *tantas componere lites*, in which a strife of cold policies and warring personalities was inextricably interwoven. In the sequel, Foliot did not escape blame for Becket's murder, nor did he, two years later, fail to be an object of attack to those who saw in him once more an aspirant to the primatial see.

Those who wish to estimate the character and influence of Gilbert Foliot will do so best by studying the whole range of his correspondence. They will find throughout a singular consistency of thought and action. Foliot was not many-sided, as was Henry of Winchester; he does not figure as patron and connoisseur, or as a great builder. His first appearance in England shows him as a zealous, even rigid, churchman, with a high ideal of religious discipline and a clearcut conception of the relations of Church and State, and of the sphere covered by the authority of the papacy and canon law. We recognize in him one of the school of Alberic of Ostia and Matthew of Albano. In English history he is of significance as the greatest of that group of able bishops, which included Robert of Hereford, Hilary of Chichester and Bartholomew of Exeter, who were used by the Roman Curia to apply to England the system of papal courts delegate, which the legateship of Henry of Winchester and the teaching of Theobald of Canterbury had introduced into the country. We can trace him throughout the years as abbot, as diocesan, as judge delegate acting with strength, perseverance and principle in private cases, in monastic questions, in disputes between Cistercians and black monks, in matters of diocesan organization. His letters, without possessing the naked realism and power of Lanfranc's, are objective, lucid and unhesitating, and if they lack the deep spiritual ardour of Anselm and Bernard, they are equally distant from the rhetoric and verbiage of Osbert of Clare and Peter of Blois. Foliot was the friend of all religious who came to him for aid, the just arbitrator in innumerable disputes, and the long affair of Cerne shows with what loyalty and persistence he could support a cause which he had made his own. Nor should it be forgotten that though he was a Cluniac of the school of Matthew of Albano, he was yet the friend of Cistercians, and a kindly host to Ailred of Rievaulx, who dedicated to him his sermons on Isaiah in an introductory letter in which he addresses the bishop of London with exactly that measure of respect and restraint which might have been anticipated. Gilbert himself, in old age, composed a commentary on the Canticle which he dedicated to his kinsman at Hereford; it is a cold and correct exercise, lacking entirely the mystical insight and the doctrinal value of Bernard's *Sermons*.

In his personal life Foliot had been from his youth upright and ascetic; in this, as in more than one trait of his character, we are reminded of another great High Churchman, Henry Edward Manning, once archdeacon of Chichester, and later cardinal; he was essentially measured, correct, and well-bred; we can therefore well appreciate the distaste with which he must have regarded alike the sudden rise and the seemingly violent impulses and swerves of Becket. But in almost every letter and recorded action there is an element of rigidity and a spirit which, while never superficial or secular, is yet formal, dry and external, not a little resembling that of the great Scots judges of the golden age of Edinburgh, and which never touches the deeply human and deeply spiritual depths of Bernard and Ailred. It is, indeed, not hard to understand how he, the righteous man of so many years' experience of government, with a fixed and reasoned conception of high policy, could fail at a moment of unexpected and intense crisis, and amid the play of violent passions, to see that a vital spiritual issue had suddenly emerged and was at stake.

IX

TWO GREAT ABBOTS:
ODO OF BATTLE AND
SAMSON OF BURY

Odo (d. 1200), an Anglo-Norman monk of Christ Church, Canterbury, became cathedral prior in 1167 and in 1175 was appointed abbot of Battle. In 1184 the monks of Canterbury put him forward as candidate for the archbishopric, but the king and the other bishops preferred Baldwin of Worcester.

Samson (1135–1212), an Englishman, was abbot of Bury St Edmunds from 1182 till his death. His name has been made familiar by Thomas Carlyle's selection of him as a type of medieval ruler in 'Past and Present'. Our knowledge of his personality is due entirely to the chronicle of one of his monks, Jocelin of Brakelond.

THE figure of Odo of Battle is one of the most attractive of all those that appear in the literature of the time; he stands almost alone among his contemporaries as an inheritor of the spirit of Lanfranc and Anselm, and may be taken as the last abbot of whom any adequate account exists who belongs to the tradition of Bec and Normandy rather than to that of Samson and the great English administrative abbots of the late twelfth and early thirteenth centuries. It is thus all the more remarkable that he should have been a monk, and filled the office of prior, at Christ Church, a house above all others exposed to contact with the world and strife of all kinds. For when all allowance is made for *esprit de famille* on the part of the Battle chronicler, the impression given is still of one who both in his private life and in his acts of government set spiritual things before temporal and suited his actions to his profession. The chronicler records that at Battle he lived among his monks as one of them, present in the church at the Offices, eating in the common refectory and reading in the cloister with the rest during the day; he would even have slept in the common dormitory but for a physical disability. He was a man of unusual eloquence, deeply read in spiritual literature, and he willingly spoke to his monks and the people, to the former in Latin or French, to the latter in English. He was also a man of great charm of character, joined to administrative ability of a high order, and it was perhaps a real misfortune for the Church in England that the bishops succeeded in quashing the attempt made by the monks of Canterbury to elevate him to the primacy in 1184. Battle, during the twelfth century, was indeed fortunate in its abbots; had others cultivated the simplicity and sobriety of Odo the subsequent history of the monastic order in England would have been happier and more peaceful. It is to be regretted that the chronicle of Battle ends early in Odo's reign; from another source we know that he left behind him a reputation of sanctity and was in some quarters counted as a saint.

The name of Odo is familiar only to a few students, that of Samson of Bury to all lovers of English literature. Probably, indeed, Samson is the single English abbot of the later Middle Ages of whom there is widespread knowledge among his countrymen, and in consequence he is still generally regarded as the type of a whole age of religion, and as the finest example of a class. Such an impression is due, apart from the accident of Carlyle's genius, to the rediscovery of his history at a moment when English sentiment, after several centuries of mistaken antipathy, and a shorter period of romantic admiration, was prepared to be more tolerant and more sane in its attitude towards the monastic life, and was delighted to find in Samson one whose worth and capability were unmistakable and shown in ways and with regard to matters with which men of every century and shade of belief are conversant; who made no demands, as does a saint and above all a saint of the monastic life, upon the reader's own powers of spiritual insight. In more recent years here, as in all other departments of medieval history, a more sophisticated and critical, if perhaps less warmhearted, attitude has been adopted, and it has been recognized that Samson, though truly great as a man of many activities and as a ruler, was not a monk of the purest type—was not, in fact, a great spiritual power, still less a saint. He is, indeed, not at all typical of the monastic centuries that preceded his epoch, still less their brightest exemplar; he is, at least as known to us from the pages of Jocelin, no more than an able administrator, a firm and just governor, and an upright, God-fearing man, and such have not been wanting to any profession or in any age. He is, however, an excellent representative of his own class in his own age, and since the process of crystallization which had developed so rapidly in the English monasteries was almost complete by 1200, he is also a true elder brother of the best and ablest abbots of the succeeding centuries. There were many Samsons between the reign of John and the Dissolution; it is not easy to find an Ailred or an Anselm.

Jocelin's *Chronicle* has achieved a world-wide celebrity in the pages of Carlyle; it is a celebrity not without its drawbacks, for what is in truth no more than a sketch of the superficies of a single type of monastic life at a single house during a particular epoch has been taken by the general reader to represent the whole of medieval monasticism. Despite this, one familiar with all the chronicles of the eleventh and twelfth centuries will probably allow Jocelin's fame to be deserved, for though the Battle chronicler has a loftier sense of his vocation, and Marleberge of Evesham a more connected and unusual story to tell, while the school of St Albans paints a richer and more varied canvas, yet Jocelin's keen personal observation and the moral worth of his hero give a unity to his diffuse records, and his work remains the only one which gives a clear picture of everyday life in a black monk monastery, as seen from the standpoint of the average monk. Even if the comparison sometimes drawn between Samson and Johnson be considered fantastic, Carlyle was right in thinking Jocelin and Boswell to belong to the same family; both have, together with keen sight and retentive memory, at once a just estimate of true worth and a *naïveté* when relating the words and actions of themselves and others which is the best guarantee of fidelity. Further than this, the comparison must not be pressed. Save for a few judgments of Samson, the sayings preserved by Jocelin have none of the moral and intellectual force that distinguishes the utterances of Johnson, and though Jocelin may well have been a better man than Johnson's biographer, Boswell was possessed of great mental sympathy and receptivity, wholly lacking in Jocelin, which go far to disguise in his pages the moral weakness of his character as we know it to have been. None of the conversation preserved by Jocelin deserves to live in virtue of any intrinsic excellence; it is merely the ephemeral stuff that passes in any group of men; its only value is that it shows us in photographic detail what otherwise could be reconstructed but vaguely in the imagination, and presents us with a glimpse of the daily life that is elsewhere concealed behind the conventional language of the typical letter-writers and chroniclers.

The Bury of Samson, as shown to us by Jocelin, is a corporate body which has taken firm and deep roots in the material and social world around it, and has adopted in much of its life the standards and aspirations of its environment. It is not rising, or being drawn, to some higher, spiritual goal, as were Bec,

Clairvaux, Rievaulx and Witham. The circumstances which differentiate its religious sentiment from that of the common experience of the modern world—the prophetic dreams of the monks, the reputed miracles of St Edmund—are, whatever we may think of their objective truth, in the order of the marvellous, not in that of the spiritual. Whenever we see Jocelin and his contemporaries acting, speaking or reflecting, it is in a wholly human manner—part admirable, part petty, all comprehensible. It may indeed well be that in Jocelin's pages the picture takes a more ludicrous and infantile appearance than the existing reality would have shown; there must have been at Bury more than one of greater intellectual power and of deeper spiritual vision than the chronicler himself; there was undoubtedly in the community a strong core of honesty and good purpose, for they chose as abbot a strong and good man who had never striven to ingratiate himself with others, and in such cases the electors must be allowed to deserve the ruler whom they receive. To characterize Bury as an abode of mediocrity would therefore be unjust, if by mediocrity is understood all lack of enthusiasm or endeavour. Yet it would be true to say that, so far as can be seen, the purely spiritual ideal of the monastic life had been lost to view, and *esprit de corps* had come to occupy for many the position of a leading interest in life and guide of action. From this respectability the figure of Samson emerges, not in virtue of a more intense or spiritual ideal, but by reason of the native force and goodness of the man; the careful reader of Jocelin will observe that though he sometimes displays love of domination and arrives at his end by aid of finesse or cajolery, Samson's years of office are (so far as we see them) conspicuously free from acts of mere selfishness or high-handedness such as could seriously affect the welfare of individuals among his subjects, and such as occur in the records of the lives of several of the ablest of his contemporaries and successors. His government, though on occasion stern and even arbitrary, was always directed to the well-being of the governed, considered not only in the mass, but as individuals, and though Jocelin's *Chronicle*, which ceases some years before the abbot's death, gives the impression that his conduct became more arbitrary as the years advanced, another source testifies that he retained the love and even the veneration of his sons unimpaired at the moment of his death. Familiar as may be the picture drawn of Samson by his chaplain, no account of English monastic life would be complete without it:

Abbot Samson was of medium height; his head was almost entirely bald; his countenance was neither round nor oval. He had a prominent nose, thick lips, eyes of glass-grey with a penetrating regard, ears wonderfully sharp, and shaggy eyebrows which he shaved frequently. A little cold made him speedily hoarse. At the time of his election he was forty-seven years of age, and had been a monk for seventeen; he then had a red beard with few white hairs in it, and fewer among the black hairs of his head, but before fourteen years were out he became white as snow in beard and hair.... He was extremely temperate and active and strong, and loved to go on horseback or on foot until age got the better of him; when he heard say that the Cross had been taken and Jerusalem lost he began to wear drawers of haircloth and a shirt of the same and to abstain from flesh-meat; he desired however that meat should be put before him at table, to increase the quantity of his alms. He preferred sweet milk and honey and such like things to any other food. Liars, drunkards and great talkers he hated, and he judged severely those who murmured at their meat and drink, especially if they were monks.... He was eloquent in French and Latin, attending rather to the order and matter than to fine words. He could read the Scriptures in English most attractively, and was wont to preach in English to the people in the dialect of Norfolk, where he was born and bred.... When abbot he gave the impression of pre-ferring the active life to the contemplative, for he praised good obedientiaries rather than good cloistered monks, and he rarely expressed approval of anyone for his knowledge of letters only, unless he had a knowledge of affairs of the world; when he happened to hear of a superior who had resigned his charge and become an anchorite he had no praise for him.... He acted also as I have never seen another act, that is, he had a great affection for many without ever or at least without frequently showing it in his countenance.

X

HUGH OF LINCOLN

St Hugh of Lincoln (? 1135–1200), a Frenchman of noble family from Avalon in Burgundy, became a Carthusian at the Grande Chartreuse and was sent to be prior of the recently founded Charter-house of Witham in Somerset. Greatly admired by Henry II he was appointed bishop of Lincoln in 1186, where he was responsible for the early Gothic rebuilding of the Norman cathedral.

HUGH OF AVALON was prior of Witham for some six years only. In the early summer of 1186, at the instance of the king, he was elected to rule the vast diocese of Lincoln which, even when shorn of Cambridge and Ely, stretched from Grimsby to Eton and from Oxford to Huntingdon, and which had been vacant, save for twelve months, for almost twenty years. But even when bishop, Hugh counted for much to Witham. To the end of his life he returned annually thither for a month or more, choosing for his visits the late summer, when he could dismiss his household to their own homes to help in gathering the harvest. At his old Charterhouse he lived in a cell like the rest and, as Wulfstan had done at Worcester a century before, took his turn as priest of the week, and used all the Carthusian vestments. Besides these long annual visits, and the celebrity which his prestige and reputation gave to his old home, Hugh seems to have retained to the end some kind of authority over Witham, for there is record of his deposing a prior, of his refusing to allow admissions and of his having a lay brother as his attendant at Lincoln.

The first Carthusian, and the last, to occupy an English see, Hugh retained as much of his old habit of life as was compatible with his new duties, and devoted all his energy to the spiritual functions of his office, refusing steadfastly to enter with his colleagues into the political life of the country. In consequence, his tenure of office left no mark on the external framework of Church history; his moral influence upon his wide and neglected diocese eludes assessment for other reasons. He did not, however, stand wholly outside the currents of life of the time. His relations with Henry II, for the short space that remained of his reign, were intimate, and he had almost equally close contact with Richard, when the king was in England or Normandy. He sought and obtained many of the best and most learned of the clergy of the new model for posts of teaching and administration at Lincoln and up and down the diocese. It also fell to him to take the decision of rebuilding his cathedral on a grand scale and in the new style, and his edifice at Lincoln, of which the transepts still remain, was the earliest work of such magnitude to be built in pure Gothic. His judgment and integrity soon singled him out as an ideal papal delegate, and between 1190 and 1200 he was constantly employed on judicial commissions, sitting at least once on the same board as Samson of Bury. In his first years at Lincoln he must have often met the aged Gilbert of Sempringham, but no record of their intercourse survives save Hugh's sanction of a modification of the lay brothers' constitutions. Chance also threw across his path at Lincoln the two writers of the age who are at once the most representative of a new school and the most familiar to the modern reader, Walter Map, archdeacon of Oxford, and Gerald de Barri, the latter of whom wrote a life of the bishop soon after his death.

Hugh was more fortunate in another biographer, Adam, a monk of Eynsham who had been his constant companion for years and who had absorbed, with his intellect at least, much of his master's spirit and doctrine; his *Life* gives a clear and living picture of the great bishop. Different as he was alike from Wulfstan, from Ailred and from Gilbert, with an order and lucidity of mind that are often reckoned characteristics of the French race, and with a quality of soul which his contemporaries loved to describe by the word 'milk-white', Hugh was a saint indeed, as every page of his life testifies—that is, he was one who appeared to those who knew him best as a pure reflection of Christ, and as such able in a strength not his own to transcend the limits of human virtue and endurance. Though a devoted and typical Carthusian, he was in a sense a Carthusian of the second generation. A lover of absolute solitude and silence, he is yet in no way a reincarnation of the spirit of Egypt or Syria; there is not even in his character a resemblance to the saints of the forest of the previous century. He was by nature and vocation a man of action and an ascetic rather than a pure contemplative, and his singularly clear conception of Christian holiness found ready expression in his teaching as bishop. He had, says his biographer, absorbed most perfectly the sanity and humility inculcated by the founders of the Charterhouse, and attached little importance to prodigies and miracles. He related such as occurred in the lives of the saints and reverenced them, recounting them to others where they might help those who admired such things; for himself, the essential holiness of the saints alone served for miracle and example. In place of wonders, he had the constant and intimate sense of his Maker's presence, and of the marvellous and unsearchable variety of his mighty works.

Though a Carthusian, Hugh could admire and respect the traditions of other and less austere orders; he had no illusions as to the essence of the teaching of the gospel. Layfolk, wondering at his sanctity, not infrequently complained to him of the hindrances they found to the service of God in the world. His reply was always the same:

Others (he said) besides monks and hermits will possess the kingdom of God. When God judges you he will not chide you for not being an anchorite or a monk, the charge against those who are found wanting will rather be that they have not been true Christians. Three things are demanded of a Christian; if one of these is lacking to a man when he is judged, the name of Christian will have no power to protect him; indeed, the name without the practice will rather prejudice than protect, for falsehood is the more atrocious in one who makes profession of the truth. Love in the heart, truth on the lips and chastity in the body: these a man must have to be in truth and in act a Christian.

And he would go on to say that the married, without changing their vocation, might share in the glory of chastity and receive a crown of reward along with virgins and those wholly continent. He himself, as bishop, had no scruple in following common usage and admitting married women and widows to sit at his table; his biographer tells how he would sign their foreheads with the cross as they knelt before him, and gently press their heads between his two palms. 'God', he would say, 'well deserves to be loved by women, for he did not shun to be born of a woman. Marvellous and precious was the privilege he thus gave to all women; it was not granted to a man to be or to be called father of God, but it was given to a woman to bear God.'

The detailed account of Hugh's last visit to his own people in Grenoble, and to his early homes, both earthly and monastic, is full of interest; still more intimate is the account of his last days and death in London. There he lay ill for long before the end, and two months before he died received Viaticum and the last anointing. When the Host was brought into the room where he was lying, 'He rose from his bed, clothed in his hair-shirt, habit and cowl, with bare feet, and kneeling, prayed and adored for long.' After he had received the two sacraments he said to those about him:

Now my doctors and my diseases may fight it out as they will, I shall have little care for either. I have given myself to God; I have received him, I will hold him and rest fast in him; it is good to abide fast in him, it is a blessed thing to hold him; he who receives him and gives himself to him is safe and sound.

Among those who visited him during those weeks were King John and Hubert Walter; to neither did Hugh give any cause for self-congratulation. The king, who sat long by his bedside, was full of kind words, but Hugh knew that little trust could be put in him and wasted none on him in return. Hubert Walter, after offering to do anything in his power for his sick colleague, felt called upon to suggest that Hugh might wish to beg pardon for any hard or provocative words or actions of which he might have been guilty, and specifically with regard to his primate. Hugh replied that he remembered well enough the occasions the archbishop had in mind, and his only regret was that the words had not been stronger. He added that he had often been weak and complaisant through human respect; should he be restored to health he would endeavour to remedy the failing. Among his last visitors was Geoffrey de Noiers, the architect in charge of the works at Lincoln. Hugh urged him to complete the altar of St John the Baptist, that it might be ready for a large gathering shortly to take place at Lincoln, and to have it consecrated at once. He had hoped to do this himself; that was not to be, but he would be among those present at the gathering he had spoken of. The gathering was for his funeral, and his body was laid by the altar of St John, where it remained till his presbytery was taken down to make room for the Angel choir and for the feretory in which his relics reposed until the Reformation.

Hugh died in 1200, but there is every indication that Witham remained as he had formed it for some decades after his death, and that it passed beyond the limits of our period as a house which not only observed in their fullness the statutes of the Charterhouse, but which was a spiritual magnet attracting to itself a strong, if small, body of ardent life. It was the last, and in some ways the purest, of those successive waves of fresh monastic life which had drawn from France and broken upon the English shore. If this account of Witham and St Hugh has seemed disproportionately long, it may at least have served as an attempt to atone for the neglect that has overtaken the place with the passage of the centuries, and to call attention to a spot which was for a period one of the centres of the spiritual life of England. The numerous visitors to Rievaulx, to Fountains and to Tintern, to St Albans and St Edmundsbury, see at least some material traces of the habitations of the monks, and give at least a passing thought to their life, but only a mound—if even so much—marks the site of the cloister built by Hugh of Avalon, the scene of so many meetings between the great bishop of Lincoln and Adam of Dryburgh, and few of the many who pass by the place in the great expresses to or from the west realize, as their glance falls upon the unpretentious roof and small turret of Witham church, that they are looking upon all that remains of the first Charterhouse of England, and the home of the last of a long line of sainted monk-bishops.[1]

[1] The name, Witham Friary, which the place bears, is not a modern misnomer, but a survival of the primitive style; the Carthusians were known as *fratres*.

XI

GERALD OF WALES

Gerald of Wales (Giraldus Cambrensis, ? 1146–1220) of distin-
guished Anglo-Welsh descent, divided his long life as a cleric
between administrative work in Wales, periods of study and
writing, and litigation in England and Rome. He was twice
disappointed in his hopes of attaining to the see of St David's. He
wrote much, chiefly about himself and church life in England and
Wales. His best-known work, the 'Journey through Wales
(Itinerarium Cambriae)' describes his experiences in the company
of Archbishop Baldwin, who preached the Crusade in Wales in
1188.

GERALD OF WALES is probably of all the writers of the twelfth
century the one most familiar to English readers, and he has
been consistently fortunate in the friends he has found among
editors and biographers. His excursion into the realm of Irish
history and ethnology has ensured to him celebrity of one
kind, and it so happens that of his other works, the book in
which his amiable qualities appear to the best advantage and
his failings are inconspicuous is one which by reason of its
subject has appealed during the last century to innumerable
lovers of the beauties of Wales. Gerald de Barri belongs to
that small class of writers which counts in its ranks the illus-
trious name of Cicero and is made up of those to whom the
world listens most readily when they speak about themselves.
Vain and naïve to a degree, he provides us in his pages with a
whole arsenal of weapons with which to attack him, yet he has
always succeeded in exciting in his readers an interest which
has in it more of affection than dislike. He is, indeed, a
medieval member of the fraternity to which belong Cellini

and Pepys and Creevey, and has the peculiar advantage of having written in an age of which the abundant literature is for the most part serious, formless and colourless; his extreme facility, his vivacity, and his love of anecdote have therefore all the charm of contrast. He has besides a number of characteristics which give him a kinship with the modern world: a love, or at least a sense, of natural beauty and wild landscape; a warm affection for his home and for his native land; a keen memory for friendships that had meant much to him in the past; a curiosity for the marvellous and the uncanny; a ready, if often ineffectual, aspiration towards the ideal; and a genuine admiration for nobility of character. It may be added that these qualities, as has already been suggested, are seen at their best in the two or three books which are most readily accessible in translation and which deal with subjects of general interest; in much of his later work the facility becomes mere fluidity and utter formlessness, and the love of anecdote sheer sculduddery.

Gerald's life was one of movement, disturbance and controversy, and it put him in a position to know well many of the most eminent figures of his day; he was, indeed, acquainted with the kings Henry II, Richard and John; the archbishops Hubert Walter, Baldwin and Stephen Langton; Hugh of Lincoln, Innocent III, Walter Map and many others. In the final event, his was a life of disappointment, frustration and waste, and this declension is unquestionably reflected in his works. The writings of his early days, before the death of Henry II, have in them freshness and generosity of appreciation; then came the years of adventure and strife, and the books that deal with them have a tinge of strain and bitterness, and all is regarded from the angle of a personal quarrel; the keen observer of earlier years is still there, but he is no longer tolerant and receptive. Finally, the last books, and in particular the *Speculum Ecclesiae*, fall in tone below the level demanded of any serious work of history or criticism; the chapters flow out like water from a spring, or like the words of a man talking to himself with little or no inflexion of the voice, and the matter is as fluid as the manner. Yet even here Gerald's gift of vivacity does not wholly desert him; the reader may at times feel indignation, or disgust, but his attention is held; Gerald never falls into mere dullness.

When the historian comes to assess the value of Gerald's arraignment of contemporary monasticism a kind of paralysis invades him; he has a sense that he is hunting in a nightmare or grappling with wraiths. For to suppose that Gerald had the intention, similar to that of a later reformer or modern critic, of arraigning the monks of his time before the bar of the world's or posterity's judgment, is to attribute to his mind a consistency and a purpose which it did not possess. He was but a keen, critical, perhaps we may even feel at times a morbid, spectator; he had moved for the greater part of his manhood in the circles of courts and schools whither gravitated all that was least settled in the intellectual life of the times, and where numberless acute minds, perpetually witnessing the intrigues of ecclesiastics and serving as a clearing-house for all scandals, were unhindered in all that they said or wrote by any responsibility of office or by the standards of sobriety which common consent, sanctioned by law, has imposed upon all who publish books at the present day. His criticisms, therefore, like those which a wronged or wounded man utters in private conversation, are often thrown out with no ulterior purpose whatsoever.

Beyond this, it is almost always singularly difficult to grip one of Gerald's stories and (to use the phrase) nail it to the counter. When is he telling the exact truth concerning an incident of which he has himself been witness? When is he recording a mass of hearsay accretions which have crystallized round a core of fact? When is he merely retailing a legend so remote from the facts as to be little more than a *fabliau* or a *ben trovato*? On occasion the reader can be tolerably certain of the answer to such questions; more often he is forced to leave the anecdote in a kind of penumbra which conceals the boundaries of fact and fiction.

With regard to the black monks, the first and on the whole the most severe charges are brought against the cells where only a few monks, or even only a single individual, were in residence. Here it is probable that facts went far to justify the indictment. These small country priories and cells, unorganized as monasteries and accomplishing no work for the Church, had no sufficient spiritual *raison d'être*; inevitably their personnel was inferior, and their observance incomplete; under such conditions worse would often follow.

After the cells, Gerald criticizes the rich diet of the black monks. Excess in matters of food and drink has always formed a wide and attractive target for satirists from Lucilius and Juvenal to Dryden and Swift. Eighty years before Gerald wrote, the topic of Cluniac meals had supplied material for some of Bernard's most brilliant pages; the monastic good cheer was to continue as a commonplace until the Reformation and beyond, and the evidence of the chronicles of the twelfth century shows that in many, perhaps in most, of the great black monk houses the food was varied and doubtless excellently cooked, and that a hierarchy of feasts had been established with extra pittances and rounds of wine. It does not, however, strengthen Gerald's case that in a book not completed in 1215 he should take as his three palmary examples an incident at Christ Church in 1180, another at Winchester of the same date, and a third, apparently at Hereford, which may indeed rest upon a substratum of truth, but which reads like an adaptation of the fourth satire of Juvenal.

After gluttony, incontinence. In this matter Gerald presents his readers with a few highly coloured stories concerning individuals, almost always unnamed, and a number of general charges. Thus after describing the worldly and luxurious life of an unnamed abbot, in language which reads like a romance, he goes on to insinuate unnatural vice, and continues to give in great detail, but with no names, two cases of this. He then passes to a consideration of the misdeeds of the three abbots of Evesham, Bardney and Westminster, who were deposed by the legate Nicholas of Tusculum; in the case of Evesham, which can be checked from Marleberge's narrative, he is substantially correct, though he gives no adequate account of the previous history of Roger Norreys or of the detestation with which he was regarded by the communities of Christ Church and Evesham; of the other two he tells us nothing definite. It must indeed be confessed that Gerald's method of procedure is in effect more odious than he perhaps intended, for he insinuates that depravity was widespread, whereas the chronicles and other literature of *c.* 1200 allow no such general judgment to be passed, and while during his lifetime his attacks were read by a few friends only, they are at the present day in the hands of all interested in medieval history. We have, therefore, no contemporary rejoinder to his strictures, and few are sufficiently familiar with all the sources to criticize them adequately for themselves.

He proposes as a remedy the institution of a system of chapters and visitation, preferably by the Ordinary, on the Cistercian model. The suggestion was not original; as has been seen, it was familiar in Curial circles and was the goal at which Innocent III consistently aimed, and no doubt was a commonplace in all gatherings of clerks. Gerald undoubtedly exaggerates the probable efficacy of the system, while he ignores the causes, legal and historical, lying behind the instances of exemption which he so deplores. Nor does he seem to have reflected that the principal cases of scandal to which he refers were the outcome of the general antinomian struggle for independence of which his own assertion of metropolitan rights at Menevia was such a striking instance. In the event, he lived to see and welcome the application of the visitation system to the black monks.

With regard to the white monks, Gerald's judgments are in some important respects different from those he pronounces on the black. In the first place, as he himself remarks, the Cistercians had no cells, which were always a special object of his attack; next, they were in possession of visitatorial and legislative machinery of whose efficacy he himself had made more than one reassuring test. Consequently, though some of his bitterest abuse is directed to the address of individual Cistercians of whom he had at one time or another fallen foul, there can be no question but that on the whole the white monks fare better at his hands than the black. If we set on one side the many stories of the misdeeds of Welsh abbots and the tale of his own wrongs, of which the whole litany from William Wibert to the lost library is rehearsed anew more than once, and do not take too seriously some anecdotes of Cistercian good cheer, the head and front of their offending is avarice, which leads only too often to injustice. To own fair acres in the neighbourhood of an abbey of the white monks, so Gerald gives his reader to understand, was to invite a repetition of the history of Naboth's vineyard, and he quotes more than once the appropriate line of Virgil. As Whitland did by Tallach, and Strata Florida by a poor nunnery under Plynlimmon, so did Aberconway by the simple culdees of Beddgelert. Sometimes even the brood preys on itself, and he tells us of the absorption of Trescoit by the rich Dore and of the persecution of Neath by Margam; more often parish churches are left desolate by the white monks. How far the particular stories, and the interpretation put upon them, are merely the issue of scandal or jealousy, it is quite impossible to determine. The Cistercians were excellent farmers, as all contemporaries admit and as Gerald himself in more than one emphatic passage asserts, and, as modern commercial life has repeatedly shown, it is not always easy to distinguish between the jealous complaints of inefficient competitors and the charges of real injustice brought against an all-powerful syndicate or a multiple-branch store. Gerald, we may think, like the children in the market-place, is not easy to satisfy: the black monks are a scandal to him by reason of their inefficiency, the white by their sound business methods. To modern readers in particular, too long familiar with a countryside where agricultural prosperity is a thing of the past,[1] the picture so often given in his pages of the smiling, rich and well-ordered fields and pastures, which gave to the environs of a Cistercian abbey the appearance of a rose of Sharon in the desert, outweighs the charge of adding field to field, and although today we may feel deeply the loss of the smallest fringe of woodland, it is difficult to accept as a crime the deforestation of three hundred acres of a remote Herefordshire valley in the twelfth century, even though its sylvan charms and sporting possibilities are set out in some of the most vivid pages that Gerald ever penned.

Yet for all his accusations and abuse, some of which is indeed harsh enough, and although he asserts more than once that the white habit has become black as soot with stains that resist all the fuller's art and the strength of the most mordant lye, Gerald retains a very deep reverence for the white monks and an earnest hope that all may yet be well. Whether this is merely the outcome of a desire to witness to the truth, or whether he never wholly forgot the pleasant associations of

[1] These words were written in 1935.

82

the distant past, and old friendship and kindnesses at Margam and Strata Florida, we cannot tell. Whatever the motive, the fact remains, and one of the most eloquent and sincere passages in the *Speculum Ecclesiae* is a prayer that the alms and works of charity of the Cistercians may even now bring about an outpouring of grace that shall leave the order in the snow-white purity of its origins. Indeed, the more carefully his pages are studied, the stronger is the impression received that essentially the white monks were still true to the spirit of prayer, work and charity, and that Gerald realized this and wished to record it, as he recorded many times the vigilance and success of their system of discipline.

Besides his charges against the monks, Gerald makes one or two general judgments of considerable interest. Thus he states (or perhaps introduces another as stating) that the black monks on the Continent are far more remiss than their English brethren, while, on the other hand, the French Cistercians are stricter than the English. He adds as an incontrovertible fact that the monks who come from France to cells belonging to their abbeys are far worse offenders against their Rule than English monks in cells. Here, as always, it is not easy to say whether Gerald is giving his mature and settled opinion. Probably, in this case, he is; probably, also, his opinion is tolerably correct. The reader will have had ample opportunity of forming a judgment on the black monks; as regards the Cistercians, no student of English monastic history in the twelfth century can have failed to remark on a certain absence of distinction in the annals of the white monks, with the important exception of the houses north of the Humber and the Ribble, with which Gerald had no first-hand acquaintance.

Gerald never wavers in his admiration for the Carthusians, and he has a predilection (shared by Henry II) for the order of Grandmont, though in his account of the origins and constitutions of these he shows the same lack of exact information as in his narrative of the origins of Cîteaux. He has besides some characteristic personal likings. He had lived at Lincoln when Hugh of Avalon was bishop, and although there is nothing to show that he had close or indeed any personal relations with the saint, he must have had numberless opportunities of speaking with his entourage. It is therefore somewhat surprising that his brief life of St Hugh, though unexceptionable in tone, should be a colourless piece of work which adds little to our knowledge either of the saint or of his biographer. More personal is his persevering memory of Baldwin's early kindness, repeated during their Welsh tour and never forgotten, though from time to time Gerald lets fall derogatory expressions concerning the archbishop. His constant admiration for Henry of Winchester is less comprehensible. It is possible, though there is no explicit evidence, that Gerald himself had received some kindness at the hands of the old bishop in the mellow days at the end of his life; certainly he lavishes on him praise such as he gives to no other, though Henry's conduct in the past had offended against so many of the monastic proprieties.

Gerald of Wales, throughout his works and in all the changes of his life, remains something of an enigma, a strange compound of prejudice and perspicacity, of superficiality and insight, of vanity and zeal, of fervent aspirations and unworthy utterances. He learnt nothing and forgot nothing, and though he was seventy or more when he revised his latest writings they are as inconsistent and irresponsible as his earliest works. It is perhaps this very characteristic of irresponsibility, joined to the vivacity which never wholly forsook him, that has caused almost all who have studied his pages to extend to him an indulgence usually accorded only to the warm and hasty aberrations of youth, and to allude to his prejudices, his obscenities and his calumnies in a tone of banter. Yet Gerald must bear the responsibility of having aspersed the fair fame of a whole class of men, the majority of whom were sincerely striving to follow a high ideal, and of having done so in a way which gave those whom he attacked no means of replying, and which has poisoned the ears of countless readers in later centuries. Lightly as all profess to treat him, more than one weighty writer on monastic history has insensibly adopted Gerald's opinions and conclusions, and he has thus come to occupy among the sources of history a position of importance which is out of proportion to his worth. When all is said, it is not easy to account for his extreme animus against the monastic body. Had he himself, in his youth, felt the call to a perfect following of Christ, and chosen instead the ambitious career of preferment and celebrity?

XII

FRANCIS OF ASSISI

Saint Francis (1181/2–1226), son of a cloth-merchant of Assisi, heard the call to leave all and follow Christ in 1208. Gathering a few companions he obtained the approval of Innocent III in 1210. His 'friars' increased rapidly in numbers and became a formalized Order, probably against his original intention. He resigned the office of minister-general and, after receiving the stigmata of Christ's passion on Monte La Verna in 1224, spent the last years of his life in illness with a small group of devoted brethren; he died at Assisi in 1226 and was canonized two years later.

THE new vigour that St Francis gave to the life of the Western Church had a very different character from the stimulus given by the measures of the reforming legislators of the age. These latter sought to impose an order and a discipline upon the discordant and flaccid elements in the body of the Church by means of a legal code and measures of administration; learning, law and organization were to be the instruments of their policy; they followed a rationally calculated method of action, based on a careful study of the discipline of the past, the conditions of the age, and the external ends to be attained. Though the goal they aimed at was a spiritual rebirth, and though many of them were, like Grosseteste, men of evangelical zeal, they thought and acted as rulers and legislators in a world of men and things. St Francis moved upon another and a far deeper plane. With him, the new birth came first to his own soul; he had begun to know Christ in the reality of living by a supernatural light, not through the words of theologians and the formularies of law; he saw and followed the life of the gospel, the life of the perfect Christian, in its true simplicity

86

and fullness, not as an ideal, not as a goal, but as the only way of life. This way he gave to others: to his first companions, to Clare, to all his friars, to all the world. Francis had the mind of Christ, he lived in him, and it was an agony and ultimately an impossibility for him to divide, to adapt, and to accommodate for others the unity and fullness of his vision. Christ himself gave his teaching to the world and to the apostles with a simplicity, an elevation and a comprehensive plenitude that few or none of his hearers were capable of accepting; he left it to his followers to codify, to divide and to economize. So it was in a measure with Francis, but he was unable to give, as Christ had given, in a few strong germinal words and with the promise of divine guidance, the basis of an organization that should preserve and propagate his teaching.

He stands thus in a position apart from other founders of religious institutes in the Church; while it is true of all the saints that they have themselves lived on a different plane from others, seeing man's life *sub specie aeternitatis* with a simplicity and directness of vision withheld from ordinary men, they have as founders and legislators given to the world codes and constitutions which do not so much translate their own experience as point towards and safeguard a certain type of life. Such was the achievement of a Benedict, a Bernard, a Teresa, an Ignatius; the achievement of Francis was at once greater and less. He saw only Christ's life, in a vivid light and from a single point of view. When called upon to give to others a Rule he could only isolate certain of Christ's own words; he wrote and spoke on the spiritual, not on the forensic plane; he gave a life, not a code; and though, to those who asked in all sincerity for direction in the concrete happenings of life, he could give direct and lucid personal guidance, he was not capable of expressing in general and external legislation the principles by which his followers were to live. It was this directness and simplicity of sight and aim that at once attracted, baffled and at times exasperated those who lived and had dealings with him; the early history of the friars shows the inevitable conflict and impoverishment that took place when men of more ordinary mould strove to express his teaching in their own idiom; and modern literature, with its repeated endeavours to interpret *Francescanismo* in terms of art, of poetry, of social reform or of romance, 'still clutching the inviolable shade', bears witness to the perplexity of the human mind when confronted with one who, while intensely receptive of all beauty and sensitive to the needs of the world of creatures around him, nevertheless had bread to eat which they knew not, and walked by a light other than theirs.

The aim of Francis, which in intension was so deep and comprehensive, was in extension also simple and wide. The leaders of monastic reform in the past had either addressed themselves only to a small band of *âmes d'élite* or had proclaimed that all who sought salvation in its full security must seek it within the shelter of a monastic rule. Francis was convinced that his message was for all, for the whole world, like the message of Christ himself. He preached repentance first, and then the gospel in all its depth and purity. To this he had himself been called; this was the way which Christ himself had taught him to give to those who had been given as his followers from the world; this he gave to Clare and her sisters; this he offered to all Christians in his preaching, in the Order of Penance and in the letter which, with sublime and simple confidence and directness, he addressed 'to all Christians, religious, clerics and lay, men and women, all who lived in the whole world'. It is, however, very noteworthy that there is no trace in his sayings or writings of the tendency, which can be seen in such earlier reformers as Peter Damian, to equate the Christian life with the monastic or the eremitical. Francis, who distinguished in his own life between the stage of penance, the turning, that is, from evil, and the perfect following of Christ with its abandonment of merely human standards, made something of the same distinction between what he demanded of his friars and what he proposed to those who had no call to join him.

But of those who were so called he demanded what no religious legislator hitherto had asked, and it is this quality of intension which sharply divides his Rule from the previous monastic and canonical Rules: it is neither an external code nor a propaedeutic to perfection, but an enunciation of the pure and full imitation of Christ in certain aspects of his life. It is this insistence on purely spiritual, supernatural action, this elimination of all but the highest, not only in the framework of his institute, but in all relations between his friars and the authorities of the Church, and with men at large, that makes of the Rules and Testament of St Francis something unique among the Rules of religious orders. The founder himself saw clearly that many of his followers would fail to live on the purely spiritual plane and that authority, within and without his order, would seek to modify his demands or translate them into legal formulae. Even when full allowance is made for the embroidery of the generation after his death which, able to prophesy from the event, may have put point and clarity into some of his words, his genuine writings and the incidents of his last years make it clear that Francis foresaw that few would follow the form of perfect living that he wished to give. Hence it was that he felt called to assert, not only to individuals in private, but to all in the text of his Rules and Testament, that the right of the individual friar to follow the perfect way was indefeasible, and that obedience should not be given to commands running contrary to spiritual perfection, even if persecution at the hands of superiors were to ensue. This, as few were slow to see, was capable of misinterpretation at the hands of those who claimed licence in the name of spirituality, and Francis had perforce to make something of a verbal compromise. But from the doctrine itself he never receded; others might see and speak forensically, he could only write, as he saw, with spiritual simplicity.

Besides this note of intensity, the institute of Friars Minor came, even before the death of Francis, to have two essential characteristics which separated it from all previous orders, though they were shared to a greater or less degree by the other bodies of friars. While he made full and explicit allowance for a contemplative and solitary element in the body of his followers, Francis was always clear in his declaration that it was their vocation as a body to preach to all men, faithful and heathen alike, both by the example of a life of service lived among men, and by direct, formal, widespread evangelization. From this there followed the second distinguishing note of the friars. They formed from the first one great body, not an aggregate of communities; they were not bound as individuals to perpetual stability in a particular home, nor even to continual residence in any home; in the eyes of St Francis, the friar, like his Master, had no home, and must be prepared to spend much of his life on the road or as a pilgrim lodger; he might be sent, or might volunteer to go, anywhere in the world where souls were to be found needing to hear the gospel preached.

Besides these two characteristics, which were in a sense external, the Rule of St Francis made three essentially spiritual demands which were from the first to cause the keenest controversy and searching of heart, and which have never ceased to attract and to perplex both friars and historians throughout the centuries. These were absolute poverty, implying incapacity for even corporate ownership and a refusal of all physical contact with money as a possession; refusal to solicit or accept ecclesiastical privilege; and the renunciation of all human learning. Those who have studied the history of the religious orders in the twelfth century will have no difficulty in recognizing the accuracy with which Francis's intuition had hit upon the three great contemporary sources of spiritual corruption. The avarice and capitalization of all religious bodies; the litigation and chicanery that accompanied the struggle for privilege and exemption; the desiccation of theology, and particularly of those branches of theology concerned with Scripture and the spiritual life, and the prevalence of an arid and heartless ingenuity among the class of clerics who still held almost a monopoly of learning—these are, and must continue to be, the commonplaces of all who consider the life of the Church in the fifty years following the death of St Bernard. It is easy to see in these three demands a psychological result of the conversion and call of Francis himself, from traffic to poverty, from class warfare to the common life, from illiteracy (in its contemporary sense) to evangelization. But the practicability of these demands, as made of an organized body of men counted by many thousands, and even their desirability in all circumstances, were not so easy to grant. Ownership, and the holding of money, a position of chartered independence, a command of the learning of the centuries, these were not of themselves evil, or inconsistent with perfection of soul. As regards the first, the example of Christ himself could be, and was in the event, alleged victoriously; for the others, such recent examples of sanctity as Thomas of Canterbury and Anselm of Bec might have been put forward. Material possessions, the advantages of privilege, and the riches of the mind, though often the occasion of spiritual loss, are not in themselves evil or the cause of evil; it is not the material presence of creatures, but the desire for them, that separates from God. Yet Francis demanded of his followers these three material renunciations with inexorable reiteration, and the early history of the Friars Minor is in large part a record of the mental strife which was the outcome of attempts to reconcile departures from the letter of the Rule and Testament with fidelity to the profession of a friar.

The spontaneity, the independence and the freshness that radiate to such a unique degree from every recorded act and word of Francis have been remarked by all who have studied the sources of our knowledge of his life. They have, indeed, often been misinterpreted as if they were a shaking off of the established order of the Church, or a novel restatement of the spirit and ideals of Christianity. Such a view, in itself without any historical basis, fails to take reckoning of the spiritual, supernatural power which made Francis what he was. Free as was his spirit and antipathetic to formalism and Pharisaism of all kinds, spontaneous and original as were all his words and works, they were so because he lived and moved by a light and love simpler than law, of which Christ's teaching in the gospel record and the tradition of the Church were expressions in human words. To most men, the doctrines of the Church and her sacraments appear as means of attaining to Christ; Francis knew Christ more directly, lived in him and his sacraments, and saw in the Church the reflected beauty of God's authority. His freedom was not the freedom of revolt or escape, but of eminent simplicity, and confident self-possession.

For this very reason, the absolute freshness and originality which were characteristic of his mind had full scope. Perhaps they can be appreciated adequately only by those long familiar with the religious literature of the early Middle Ages and of the renaissance of the eleventh and twelfth centuries. Francis is, indeed, spontaneous and original on a double count;

he has neither the outlook nor the culture of the early Middle Ages. The *Weltanschauung* common to all minds in the Western Church between Augustine and Gregory VII, which is seen alike in St Benedict and Gregory the Great, in Bede and in Peter Damian, and which was in part the outcome of the collapse of the ancient civilization and the impotence of the new nations to attain mental self-possession—the outlook which saw the forces of evil as all but visible and tangible, and which regarded catastrophe and judgment as always impending upon the world—this has given place, for Francis, to a more personal, direct view, in which the human life of Christ on earth is the centre of the world's history and the model of all lives. Together with the old outlook has disappeared also the emphasis on the need for a flight from the world to the desert or at least into the bosom of a monastic society apart from the rest of men; for Francis solitude is something entirely spiritual.

Nor is there with him any trace of that literary culture which clothes even the most intimate utterances of such wholly sincere voices as those of Anselm, Bernard and Ailred. Compared with the limpid freshness of Francis, the letters and dialogues of the abbots of Clairvaux and Rievaulx seem artificial and rhetorical; they are of a school and of a date; the most characteristic utterances of Francis have something of the dateless purity of the gospels. Anselm and Ailred consciously, Bernard perhaps unconsciously, speak to the mind as well as to the spirit; Francis speaks directly to the soul.

Francis had by nature a mind exquisitely sensitive and keenly receptive of all beauty, whether of earth or sky, of colour, sound or taste, and as readily repelled by every manifestation of deformity or squalor. That this keen and unstudied love of all beauty grew throughout his life and was greatest during the last months when his body was one wound

and every sense ached is a commonplace among his biographers; it extended to all creation, flowers, trees and animals,
and was most characteristic when it found a new joy in the
elemental clarity and beauty of the most familiar things, sun,
moon and stars, earth, air, cloud and water. In its simplicity,
its purity, this faculty of Francis to seize upon the central
beauty of all creation inevitably recalls the similar, but still
purer and more comprehensive, faculty in Christ himself,
which so often passes unnoticed by reason of its extreme
directness and simplicity. Along with this went a delicacy
and intuition of sympathy hard to parallel even among the
saints. Perhaps the most revealing of all traits in Francis's
nature is his expression in terms of a mother's love of the
tireless tenderness of care which all should have for those under
their charge. His ministers are to be as mothers to their friars;
in the minute treatise on brethren in the hermitages the term
'mother' occurs no less than six times in this sense, and Francis,
who allowed and encouraged those nearest him to address him
thus, assumes the title in his most intimate address to his
beloved disciple. In this, as in all things else, he was no doubt
following the exemplar and echoing the expressions of Christ,
but it was also the revelation of a new age in Europe of which
Ailred of Rievaulx had been a harbinger half a century before;
to Francis, rather than to the centres of contemporary learning,
must we look for the fruit of the promise that had been given
by the flowering of the renaissance of humanism a hundred
years before.

A similar freshness appears on the deeper, more spiritual
plane, and in nothing, perhaps, is this seen more clearly than
in Francis's use of Scripture. It has often been remarked that
Bernard's writings are a mosaic of sentences, phrases, words,
allusions and reminiscences drawn from the inspired books,
and though a familiarity with Scripture almost as great is

found in all the lettered ecclesiastics of the day, such as Peter of Blois, Baldwin of Canterbury, and the rest, there is a sincerity and a reality in Bernard's quotation which the others lack. Yet, when compared with Francis, Bernard in his turn appears frigid, artificial and unreal. The most characteristic writings of Francis are little more than centos of passages from the gospels, but the quotations have in them nothing of art; they present the direct, not the allegorical meaning of the words; they are, indeed, not quotations from a book, however sacred, but words of life and power, words which are works, truths that have been lived. To a superficial reader it might seem that the sentences which follow one another have been assembled almost perfunctorily by a memory which had no other store of wealth, but the more thoughtful will realize very speedily that the choice of texts, their order, and the illustration that they give, reveal a spiritual vision of marvellous clarity and penetration.

And because he was conscious alike of his vision and of its clarity Francis never ceased to assert the originality of the life that he had found for himself and his friars, and to resist all attempts that were made within and without the order to pour the new wine into old bottles. When we remember how faithfully each new monastic reformer of the early Middle Ages from Benedict to Lanfranc had copied the model of the past, and how even the most clear-sighted and drastic legislators of the revival had staked their all upon reproducing as nearly as possible the practice of distant antiquity, Italian or Egyptian, the resolution of the unlettered deacon Francis, who reverenced all priests and religious as his masters, to have nothing to do with the Rule and regulations of Augustine, Benedict or Cîteaux, but to initiate a new way of following Christ in lowliness and simplicity, becomes all the more striking in contrast. To this resolution he held to the end, not only in private conference among his sympathetic disciples, but in crowded general chapter and in presence of Cardinal Ugolino.

The Friars Minor, then, according to the mind of their founder, were a new model in Christendom. The novelty of their way was to be found in its simplicity and lowliness, and also in the fact that their way of life was to have the full liberty of Christ's human life on earth. The friars were not to live, like the early monks and the later eremitical orders, wholly apart from men, nor were they to live the segregated lives of the corporate bodies, as did the black and white monks of the twelfth century, and the canonical orders in general. They were to live and work as Christ had lived and worked, now in the hidden labourer's life of Nazareth, now alone in the desert and mountains, now on the highways and in the market-places of Galilee and Judea. And this life was to be lived, this work of evangelization was to be done, as Christ had lived and preached, in actual poverty, without assured means of livelihood and without any aid from the training and learning of the schools; the friars were to be at once more free and more strictly confined than the new orders of the previous century, which had vied with each other in devising constitutional safeguards for poverty, seclusion and abstinence. The followers of Francis had the gospel freedom of eating what was set before them, and of choosing, now to preach to the infidel, now to retire to the mountain hermitage, and they were relieved of the heavy choral and ceremonial observances of a great abbey. Their superiors, in Francis's original scheme, were to be neither the permanent heads of families and the great prelates such as were the abbots, black and white, nor the impersonal directors of a vast army of effectives, but the servants and 'mothers' of groups of friars, whose only responsibilities were to be spiritual. At the same time (and only so could such freedom exist) every friar, by his act of surrender to God, committed himself to a literal and complete observance of the words of Christ commanding trust in God and the perfect following of himself; he was held also to an absolute obedience to the letter and spirit of Francis's Rule, to the commands of superiors within that Rule, and to absolute poverty. Abandonment once and for all of all material possessions; a life without care for the present or provision for the future; a readiness and desire to imitate Christ in his Passion and death—these were the three words that Francis and Bernard, his first friar, had heard before the order of Friars Minor was born,[1] and Francis continued throughout his life to realize them more completely in himself and to demand that his followers should accept them not merely as an ideal, but as the practical guiding principles of his new way for all.

This brief outline of the teaching of Francis has been given as an aid towards an appreciation of his significance in the religious history of Europe and to an understanding of some of the controversies and ideals of the English friars in the first decade of the province. Too many, by using of Francis and his words such terms as 'mystical', 'ideal' and 'romantic', have escaped not only from the task of setting his most earnest and intimate utterances alongside the later history of his order, but also from the deeper effort involved in the comprehension of his own mind and life.

As all who have read the history of Francis know, his friars did not as a body accept, even during his lifetime, the way of life he wished to give them in all its purity. Failing for breath in the rarefied air, they fell back into the broader ways that he had of set purpose abandoned. They would not live in the

[1] The texts were Matt. xix. 21: 'Sell all thou hast', etc.; Luke ix. 3: 'Take nothing for your journey, neither...bread nor money', etc.; and Matt. xvi. 24: 'If any man will come after me, let him deny himself, and take up his cross, and follow me.'

complete poverty of resources, material and constitutional, which he required of them, and they adopted, to some extent at least, the organization and practices of earlier religious institutes. In things of the spirit elasticity and tension increase and decrease conjointly; only the heroic can be free; and thus the Friars Minor, unable to accept in full Francis's Testament, were caught up in the more complex and more rigid network of disciplinary and constitutional regulations. Yet although something of sadness hangs over the history of the Friars Minor of the second generation, the new life that Francis himself had lived and shown to others remained and remains in the Church, and has in all centuries inspired individuals and groups within his Order as the model for a type of sanctity which all recognize as Franciscan. It has, besides, enriched the spirit of all Europe, not only, or even principally, as a new manifestation of the brotherhood of all men and of the share of all creatures in the beauty and beneficence of God, but as a showing forth of the Gospel lived in its fullness with a detail and a clarity rare to equal in any age, and as a revelation of the imitation of Christ crucified, in love and suffering, which though present in essence in all Christian sanctity, appeared in Francis in a new form to which the growing mind of Europe responded at once, and which was to prove the prototype of much that was to come in the religious life of the West.

XIII

THOMAS OF ECCLESTON

Thomas of Eccleston, an English Franciscan friar of whom nothing is known save a few personal details, entered the order in 1232/3 and wrote a short chronicle describing the arrival and the early years of the Franciscans in England, which he finished in 1258–9.

FRIAR THOMAS OF ECCLESTON, the chronicler, is a valuable and indeed a unique witness, not only to the achievements of the first English Minors, but also to the existence of a world of sincere and simple English piety of which neither the chronicles of Paris nor the treatises of Bacon and Pecham give a hint. He alone shows us the leaven of Francis at work in a distant country, and among men who could have had no conception of the background of Umbrian life.

Brother Thomas, like Jordan of Giano, is happiest when telling of the simplicity and purity of the early friars, but there is in his pages no trace of the bitterness of strife or nostalgia for the bright dawn in Umbria. The stories he tells, the enthusiasm he records, are such as form part of the birth of every true religious venture; there is no trace in them of party spirit or apologetic. Eccleston himself is remarkably self-effacing; there are none of the vanities of Salimbene or the occasional naïvetés of Jordan; he gives no personal details, and when he relates incidents which he has heard of one of the actors he earns our respect by making no comment or reflection.

The most attractive parts of his narrative are, as might be expected, those that tell of the simplicity and poverty of the first friars. There is the well-known account of the first days of all at Canterbury:

Soon after this they were granted the use of a small room underneath the schoolhouse. In this they sat almost all day with the door shut, but when the boys had gone home in the evening they went into the schoolroom, made themselves a fire, and sat by it, and sometimes when they were going to have their evening drink in common they put a crock on the fire with lees of beer in it, and then dipped a porringer in the pot and drank a round, while each said something to rouse devotion. One who had the good fortune to share this holy poverty related that their drink was sometimes so thick that they poured in water and so drank it joyfully.[1]

There is the equally familiar anecdote of the young novice Salomon fitzJoyce who, as he told Eccleston, used, when returning from a begging tour, to carry flour and salt and a handful of figs for a sick brother in his cape and a bundle of wood under his arm, and who never accepted anything that was not of rigid necessity. His self-denial was such

that it happened once to him to suffer such extremity of cold as to believe that he was then and there about to die. As the brethren had not the wherewithal to make him warm, their brotherly love taught them a remedy; they all gathered round him and pressing close to him, like a litter of pigs, they made him warm.

Touches of this kind abound in Eccleston. There is his vivid account of the first recruits at Oxford, eager and high-spirited in their new adventure, with boyhood's keen sense of the ridiculous and the contagious laughter of the novitiate:

As the young friars at Oxford laughed unceasingly, a command was given that one particular brother should receive the discipline as often as he laughed in choir or at table. Now it happened, when he had received the discipline eleven times in a single day, but still could not contain his laughter, that he dreamt one night that the whole community was in choir as usual, and as usual the friars felt an inclination

---

[1] Cerevisia of this kind was more like porridge than modern beer.

to laugh, when lo, the image of the Crucified which stood by the door of the choir turned to them as if alive, and said: 'These are the sons of Korah who laugh and sleep when I am on the cross', and it seemed to him that the Crucified strove to loosen his hands from the cross as though fain to come down and be off.... When this dream was told, the brethren were dismayed and bore themselves with greater dignity and without excessive laughter.

As a pendant to this picture of Oxford may be set another from Cambridge, where in the friars' minute chapel on the feast of St Laurence,

although there were only three friars who were clerks, that is to say, Br William of Ashby and Br Hugh of Bugton and a novice called Br Elias who was so lame of his legs that they had to carry him into the chapel, they nevertheless chanted the office solemnly with plain-song, and the novice wept so copiously that tears ran openly down his cheeks as he sang. And when he had died a holy death at York, he appeared to Br William Ashby at Northampton, who asked him how it went with him, and he answered that it went well.

So all-pervading was the comradeship of Eccleston's early days

that the only thing that could sadden them was the necessity of parting. For this reason they often accompanied departing brethren a long way on their journey, and showed their faithful and affectionate regard by tears shed on both sides as they parted.

From Eccleston's pages a whole series of vignettes can be cut: that of Agnellus, 'crying through three whole days before he died, "Come, sweetest Jesus"', who, at the last, having absolved his community and ordered them to begin the prayers for a passing soul, 'closed his eyes with his own hands, crossed his hands on his breast', and so died; or that of Vincent of Worcester, 'the father of his native city, who, stern and self-denying to himself, was so gentle and generous to others that he was loved by all as if he were an angel'; or that of the friars in general 'so assiduous in prayer that there was hardly an hour in the night when there were not some of the brethren at prayer in the chapel'.

The picture of the English province given by Eccleston is indeed a very pleasing one; no doubt he was a patriot, but his story rings true; he is telling of the examples which inspired and warmed his own endeavour, and he writes that others may share the warmth. He tells how Agnellus, going through the petty expenses of the London friary with the abstemious Salomon, became suddenly appalled at the mounting sum and threw down the rolls and tallies with a cry of anguish, though Eccleston himself, when a guest at London, then a large convent of fifty or more, had seen the brethren drinking beer so bitter that water was preferable, and eating unbolted bread. Even bread had been lacking there for a long space during his stay. At Oxford, the scene of such intense intellectual activity, and in its custody, the friars wore no shoes and were without pillows; in the custody of Cambridge at the same date they went without mantles through lack of money, and the first chapel at Cambridge, built before 1238, was of the simplest model, a few days' work for a single carpenter; in the custody of York it was never permitted for more friars to live in a house than could be supported by alms of food without incurring debts. At Gloucester, John of Malvern, visitor c. 1231, proceeded severely against the guardian and the friar who had painted a screen in the chapel; Oxford was for ten or fifteen years without a guest-room, and the walls of its infirmary were only six feet high; stone took the place of clay in the walls of the dormitory at London c. 1238. The last change took place in the days of Albert of Pisa, who caused the stone cloister at Southampton to be destroyed, despite the protests of the burgesses of the town who had presumably built it. William of Nottingham, provincial 1241–54, was unremitting in his efforts to preserve the original poverty.

At London he ordered the roof of the church to be altered and decorations in the cloister to be erased in the interests of simplicity, and at Shrewsbury he replaced the stone walls of the dormitory with walls of clay. In default of any chronicle to take up the story after Eccleston it is difficult to trace the development of domestic building among the friars, but the authority best qualified to pronounce has given it as his opinion that they remained unassuming for long, and that until 1270, if not after, the churches of the friars in England remained small and of the simplest construction.

XIV

ROGER BACON

Roger Bacon (? 1214–92), an Englishman, studied as a clerk in Oxford and Paris, where he was one of the first to lecture on Aristotle's philosophical works. Returning to Oxford, he devoted himself to natural science and mathematics under the influence of Bishop Grosseteste. Becoming a friar about 1255, he continued his scientific studies, but fell foul of the authorities of his order and was probably under some sort of restraint for a time. He died, an old man, probably at Oxford in 1292.

ROGER BACON, like almost all the great schoolmen from Alexander of Hales to Duns Scotus, eludes every attempt on the part of posterity to obtain a clear sight of his life's history and of his personal environment and intimate character. Apart from the autobiographical *obiter dicta* which are scattered all too rarely about his chaotic treatises, we know next to nothing of his life; the date of his birth, the date of his master's degree, the date of his reception to the habit and the date of his death are all uncertain. Yet it would be an error to imagine Roger Bacon (or, indeed, Adam Marsh and many other leading scholastics) as a friar of obscure and poor parentage and a narrow horizon bounded by the walls of his convent and the pronouncements of his masters in the schools. He was, it would seem certain, the son of an Anglo-Norman family of note, branches of which were settled in Norfolk, Essex and Dorset; he was possibly a nephew of the celebrated Oxford Dominican, Robert Bacon, and an elder brother held the family estates. He was born probably *c.* 1214, and certainly spent all his life from boyhood in study at Oxford and Paris; as in all likelihood he did not become a friar till *c.* 1255 no specifically Franciscan character is to be sought in his writings, though many date from after his reception and it is certain that he was influenced deeply by Grosseteste and to a less extent by Adam Marsh, Thomas of York and others of the Oxford school. There is no evidence that he ever became a doctor of theology or that he was in priest's orders.

Almost all the forty odd years of his life as a friar were spent abroad, ten of them in retirement owing to frail health accompanied, we may suspect, by some kind of neurotic disability. He had his day of glory, when he was requested to set out his programme for the reform of learning for the benefit of Clement IV, but the pontiff died before he could implement the scheme or reward its author, and Bacon's lack of self-control continued to alienate sympathy. The later decades of the century were electric with theological disputes, with upheavals among the Minors and with tense feeling between Minors and Preachers. The generals of the two orders met in Paris in 1277 to negotiate a truce, and it is probable that Bacon was thrown to the wolves he had infuriated. In any case, he seems to have spent more than ten years (1278–c. 1290) in confinement. His death probably occurred in 1292, and at Oxford.

The extraordinary reputation which Bacon acquired as a necromancer within a century of his death, and which endured for nearly three hundred years, his equally undeserved fame as a martyr to the cause of free thought, and his (probably also unmerited) celebrity as the inventor of gunpowder and the telescope, and the prophet (as Leonardo da Vinci in a later age) of many scientific and mechanical discoveries of today, have in the past attracted to him the attention, often misplaced and almost always undiscerning, which his countrymen have failed to give to his greater contemporaries in the schools of Oxford and Paris. This is not the place to attempt a survey of his achievement or to assess his mind and character, which would seem to have been vitiated by some deep psychological flaw, and by a restlessness and lack of control that prevented his brilliant talents and intuitive genius from attaining full realization. In his extreme sensitiveness, in his intolerance of the obscurantism, real or supposed, of those in high place, and in the jealous, critical temper which prevented him from receiving what his great rivals in the schools had to give, he has affinities with Abelard, with Lorenzo Valla, and with de Lamennais. Here it is only to the purpose to note that it was as a Franciscan and as the heir of the Franciscan traditions at Oxford that Bacon turned from speculative thought to pursue his encyclopaedic investigations into mathematics, natural science and the conditions of society around him. His work is at once the culmination and the last 'uncontaminated' manifestation of the peculiar characteristics of the school of Oxford—an interest in positive studies, both for their own sake and as forming a basis for theology, a close attention to observation and experiment, and an independence of outlook with regard to all the conventions of contemporary thought. The developments of later ages and the desire which few have been able to resist to compare him with his later namesake, whose position as thinker and reputation as reformer are strangely similar, and almost equally equivocal, have made Roger Bacon an object of interest to many who have known little of, and cared less for, scholastic philosophy and theology. Recent and more careful investigation has suggested that his deepest significance in the history of thought is rather the promise that his work holds, and the possibility that had other and more sober thinkers followed in his footsteps medieval philosophy might have retained that contact with the actual, the concrete and the individual which alone can keep the speculations of the pure reason living and fruitful, and might in consequence have avoided the decay that took place when thought came to be increasingly isolated from life and from the changing conditions of society.

Roger Bacon had without doubt a mind of singular intuitive genius and rare critical power. He seized with precision the basic faults in the foundation of the later scholastic method which did in the event bring about a fossilization. He deplored the divorce of pure thought from life and experience, the insecurity of the positive basis of uncritical texts, jealous tradition and bookish science on which it rested, and the neglect of the ancient heritage of form and beauty. Though he himself had few or no gifts as an artist in words, and was in no sense a literary or aesthetic humanist, he could pass a true judgment on the arts, and his criticisms of contemporary tendencies in music and his regret at the abandonment of classical prosody and metre by hymn-writers of his time are just, and have been echoed by modern judges. Moreover, when all legends have been excluded, there are still in his writings a number of remarkable anticipations of the discoveries of the Italian renaissance, and also of the general temper of mind of the humanists of the fifteenth century. It has even been said that Bacon stood for a religious culture, embracing science, philosophy and theology, which might have preserved the breadth and unity of intellectual life within the Church, and rendered the causes of the Reformation inoperative. Such an opinion is unquestionably at once an exaggeration and an undue simplification. One powerful bond of cultural union had already disappeared before Bacon's birth with the decay of the classical and literary humanism of the century between 1050 and 1150. But beyond this, when all acknowledgment has been made of Bacon's powers, as also of his fundamental orthodoxy and sense of tradition, it must be confessed that he moves altogether on a lower plane, and breathes another atmosphere from that of the greatest scholastics. It may be that Bonaventure, Albert and Thomas Aquinas made little account of some of the mental activities essential to a full human culture; but they, and especially the great Dominicans, had a sense of the majesty and reality of the body of metaphysical truth which is quite absent from Bacon; they were a summit of attainment; they were able with luminous clarity to harmonize in due subordination human truth with divine, and to see all things in a lucid order in which nature and grace, knowledge and love, action and contemplation filled up the rich whole of man's life.

Of this there is nothing in Bacon, and he had no group of disciples, and neither his philosophical nor his scientific opinions had any influence on the generation that immediately followed him at Paris though later masters of the Franciscan school at Oxford drew inspiration from him. In the history of the religious orders of England his significance lies chiefly in the evidence his career and writings give of the wide gulf that separated the purely 'student' Friar Minor from the first brethren of Francis of Assisi fifty years before.

XV

MATTHEW PARIS

Matthew Paris (d. 1259) an Englishman, monk of St Albans, is perhaps the best known figure among medieval monastic chroniclers and holds also a high place among the artists of his century. His chief work was his 'Great Chronicle' ('Chronica Majora'), which gives a vivid picture of the Europe of his day.

MATTHEW PARIS is without question the most familiar figure among the monastic writers between the Conquest and the Dissolution. His fame, which was established in his lifetime, has never suffered a serious eclipse among historians and antiquaries. He has been fortunate both in his literary remains, which have survived in magnificent manuscripts readily accessible to students, and in his critics, who have in the past almost without exception treated him with remarkable indulgence. The reasons for his popularity are not far to seek. His copious chronicles provide a mass of information about contemporary Europe and the near East which is not to be found elsewhere; they contain numerous personal details about celebrities derived from direct conversations or first-hand information, and extracts from original documents which are not known to have survived elsewhere; they are discursive and yet extremely readable. In the past, when the sources of medieval history were hard to come by and all except a very few scholars relied upon writers of a later date, historians were delighted to be able to follow, for an important period, an honest and extremely well-informed contemporary, upon whom they might rest their narrative in some such way as historians of Greece may rest it upon Thucydides. Moreover, the prejudices of Paris—his violent criticism of papal exactions, his obstructive resentment towards reformers, and even his jealousy of the friars—were precisely such as to appeal to Protestant, liberty-loving historians who nevertheless had a warm corner in their hearts for the monks.

In consequence, he has often been followed uncritically, or at least too exclusively, and it is only in recent years that something of a reaction has set in. Great, indeed, as are the services he has rendered to posterity, Paris, as a critical historian, is inferior, not only to Bede, but also to William of Malmesbury. Unlike his two predecessors, he is concerned almost exclusively with contemporary events; he never makes a critical examination of the sources of an earlier time. Nor does he, like Bede and Malmesbury, submit his material to complete digestion. His pages consist of a succession of separate topics, any number of which could be removed without affecting either the context or any other part of the book. He remains, in fact, a chronicler rather than a writer of history. It must be added that the mass of information he provides often creates the illusion that his account is exhaustive; this has led writers to follow him alike in his emphasis and in his silences. Finally, his judgments, though freely and fearlessly given, often lack both dignity and finality, and show a certain irresponsibility and a failure to co-ordinate the data he himself provides. Paris, indeed, has the defects of his qualities; his curiosity, wide interests and love of incident imply a certain lack of spiritual depth and of a sense of the true values of things. *Non omnia possumus omnes*: but a monastic historian whose time of manhood overlapped the last years of St Francis and the early maturity of St Thomas Aquinas cannot escape judgment by the highest standards of moral and intellectual achievement.

These shortcomings, however, must not be allowed to

obscure the very great merits of Matthew Paris. His tireless energy, upon which his friends remarked, maintained a copious output of literary and artistic work of a very high quality. When we set ourselves to imagine the labour of collecting, sifting, arranging, copying and illustrating the mass of material from which the final narrative was constructed, and the wide interest which rejected no happenings, however distant; when we consider the self-restraint needed to preserve a balance between the acquisition of information and its embodiment in literary form, the prevailing self-effacement of the historian and the absence of personal bias against individuals or of flattery of the great, we cannot in justice withhold our admiration for the talents and practical intelligence of the monk of St Albans. There is in Paris none of the morbid vanity of Gerald of Wales or the bitter cynicism of Richard of Devizes. His prejudices are largely those of his class and his age; they are not without a historical value of their own, for they show how a typical mind in a great and active monastery reacted to events and movements of which we can see the implications more clearly than could a contemporary. Perhaps it is not fanciful to see in Paris, not only a typical conservative of the age, but a medieval embodiment of many of the elements that have always distinguished the national character—a love of old custom and a fear of being dragooned into the unfamiliar; an instinctive dislike of foreign ways; and an interest in persons and events rather than in principles and movements.

Matthew Paris was clothed as a novice at St Albans on 21 January 1217; probably, therefore, he was born *c.* 1200. His name does not imply foreign birth or provenance, nor is there any suggestion of this in his writings. Gifted and versatile, he is one of the last of the monks to include within his scope, like a Dunstan, the whole range of letters and art.

His primary interest was contemporary history, and here he had the good fortune to meet with Roger of Wendover, the first great chronicler of the house. Him he succeeded in 1236; thenceforward till his own death he was engaged on his great work, the *Chronica Majora*, together with a briefer account and a collection of additions and *pièces justificatives*. He also put together and refashioned the existing materials for domestic history, adding an account of his own times in the monastery and thus launching the series of *Gesta Abbatum* which was to be continued for a century and a half after his death.

He soon became celebrated. Henry III when visiting St Albans sought him out, and on a well-known occasion at Westminster was at pains to call him up from the crowd and bid him write what he saw. Other public men, also, realized that their share in events could best be preserved for posterity by judicious conversations at St Albans. Nor were his gifts those of the student and artist alone. He had won the esteem and friendship of Haakon IV of Norway (*reg.* 1218–64) a personal friend of Henry III and a patron of English artists. When, therefore, the abbey of St Benet Holm on the island of Niderholm near Trondhjem was in financial embarrassment owing to the fraudulent action of an abbot who had absconded with the convent's seal and subsequently died, Haakon, *c.* 1246, sent the prior to England for help with a letter to Paris, through whose good offices the Cahorsin money-lenders in London agreed to a composition. When, a little later, the same abbey was at issue with the archbishop of Trondhjem, a papal legate advised the monks to solicit the pope for one to reform the observance of their house. This they did, and when Innocent IV ordered them to choose whom they would they asked for the dispatch of Matthew Paris. The pope assented, and in 1248 Paris duly accomplished his mission. With remarkable self-effacement he tells us nothing of his sojourn in Norway save for an escape, while saying Mass on shore at Bergen, from a stroke of lightning which struck the ship in which he had arrived a few hours before, but his visit has very reasonably been connected with an impulse given to Norwegian painting in the style of the school of St Albans. He remained less than a year, and his task was doubtless simply to pass on to the Norwegian monks the observance, domestic and liturgical, and the general tone of St Albans, rather than to act as disciplinary reformer and ruler, a position for which he had neither official authority nor temperament. He returned to his *scriptorium*, from which he was never again summoned by the duties of any other office; he died, while still at work, probably in 1259, leaving behind him a tradition of historical writing which endured at St Albans until the end of the fifteenth century.

XVI

HENRY OF EASTRY

Henry of Eastry (b. ? 1250), monk of Christ Church, Canterbury, was prior of that monastery for the unexampled span of forty-six years, dying an old man in 1331. He is an outstanding example of the enlightened 'high farming' of a boom period in English agriculture.

HENRY OF EASTRY was perhaps some thirty-five years old when he was elected prior and confirmed by Archbishop Pecham. When he took over the administration the monastery was in debt to the extent of £5000—more than the average income of two years—at a time when the archbishop was also struggling to overcome a weight of debts. He speedily showed himself an economist of the first order. By a rigid curtailment of superfluous expenses at home, by a clear-sighted and total reorganization of the administration, both in deliberation and accountancy at Canterbury and in executive action on the estates, as also by a farseeing and consistent development and exploitation of the land and its fruits, Eastry raised Christ Church from a state of insolvency to what was probably the highest level of productivity in its history.

For the first thirty years of his rule the economic current of the age was flowing in his favour. During the whole of the thirteenth century the great estates of England had been increasing the acreage of demesne land exploited directly by the owner, while rising prices at the end of the century and during the first decades of the fourteenth made this the 'golden age of demesne farming'. This enabled Eastry, despite exceptionally heavy losses from tempests and repeated demands, in the early thirteenth century, for loans and corrodies from the king, to sink his debts in fifteen years and inaugurate a period of sound and prosperous finance.

Though not neglectful of other interests, and willing to advise his friends on politics and foreign affairs, Henry of Eastry found his life's work within the limited, if large, area of the Canterbury buildings and estates. Within that little world no department escaped rationalization at his hands. Economy through the avoidance of waste and superfluity was an obvious measure, to be taken at once, probably in the first year of his priorate. It was accompanied by a development of the system of central treasury and regular audit already functioning, and by a fuller use of domestic ability in the council of seniors meeting at the chequer and the increasing employment of skilled external legal advice and advocacy in the prior's council. Eastry was no doctrinaire democrat, and such slight evidence as exists shows him to have been a ruler who held the reins firmly, but he was not by temperament a monopolist of power and could tolerate colleagues, not functionaries only, and during his period of rule the number of monks who took an active share in enlightened administration, either in the house or on the manors, was probably higher than at any period before or after.

In addition to the body of senior monks sitting at the chequer he enlisted the services of the ablest practical talent in the community by regularizing the position and enhancing the powers of the monk-wardens of the manors. The function of these officials does not directly concern us; here we need only note that it was Eastry who made them responsible for returning the revenues of their custody and who gave them in practice extensive discretionary powers of construction and repairs of farm buildings and of choice of the particular agricultural policy to be adopted in exploiting the individual manors. At the same time, the wardens were regularly consulted and strictly controlled by the council of seniors under the prior. The system, therefore, under a competent head who could guide his subordinates along the lines of an economic policy decided by himself, was probably as satisfactory as could be wished from a material point of view. While giving a lawful outlet for practical ability, it avoided the waste and personal aggrandizement of the old obedientiary system, and secured the maximum income for the monastery.

With this machinery at his disposal, Eastry was able to show himself a master of high farming throughout the large and scattered estates of Christ Church. He increased his land wisely and unceasingly, parcel by parcel, recouping himself for the purchase by the higher rent chargeable, and by careful and persevering embankment and reclamation in the Romney marshes. He increased his liquid assets by securing payment, or the option of payment, in lieu of labour services. He improved the yield of the land by a widespread and intelligent use of marling, by a partial rotation of crops, and by a careful breaking up of unused lands.

Disposing as he did of wide estates containing arable, meadowland and coarse pasture in varying proportions, lying on a variety of subsoils and including marsh, downland, river-bottoms and well-drained, airy hillsides, all controlled by a body with capital, he was able to exploit the resources of the country to the full. The account rolls show a complicated and scientific scheme of collection and sale by which corn and cheese—sometimes the whole yield of the land—were sold on the spot or at a distance with a keen watching of the market, while produce for home consumption, whenever necessary through exhaustion of local stocks, was bought elsewhere at a lower price. In other words, the scattered estates were to a large extent treated as a single administrative *bloc* and commercialized. In a similar way, the considerable wool crop was increased and rationalized by the concentration of the flocks on a few manors, notably the fresh, open pastures of Thanet and the Romney marshes, and by transhumance to other Canterbury possessions. As for the dairy produce of cows and ewes, this too was exploited. On manors where dairy-farming on a large scale was practicable, cheese-making for the market absorbed most of the milk; on small manors, and those where arable predominated, Eastry extended the system of milk-leases, hiring out the cattle to small farmers who paid cash on the expectation of the yield for the season. On other manors still, the contrary need was felt, and cows and ewes were hired in for cheese- and butter-making. The sum of all these measures under efficient central control resulted in a very considerable betterment of Christ Church revenue. When Eastry had weathered his difficult first years, rendered still more testing by a series of calamities due to vagaries of the climate, he was able to enjoy, during the first twenty years of the new century, a space of time in which his organization found its reward and gathered a rich harvest from the contemporary 'boom' in agriculture. The gross revenue, which c. 1290 averaged £2050, stood in the last year of his priorate, when conditions had already begun to deteriorate, at £2540, an increase of almost 25 per cent. The increase in the net revenue was no doubt very much greater.

Though Eastry's forte was undoubtedly economic administration, there is in him no trace of the bucolic. His reputation for a knowledge of the Scriptures finds little support from his correspondence, and there is no evidence that he had passed through the schools, but he was highly intelligent, with an incisive realist bent of mind, and with the assurance that often accompanies a limited outlook. His attendances in parliament, though apparently little to his taste, and his role as host to great ones on pilgrimage to Canterbury or on the road to or from Dover, put him *au courant* with public affairs, and he was a regular correspondent and counsellor of successive archbishops. He had entered the monastery in the days of Boniface of Savoy, and had had full opportunity of observing the policies and fortunes of the three distinguished men who followed him at Canterbury. Already in Pecham's day his unemotional, practical temper can be seen in his tactful but firm handling of the difficult old friar whose grievances against the monks had led him to threaten to leave his body for burial among his brethren away from Canterbury. Winchelsey, a determined man with a clear programme, was not a promising subject for cautious counsel, and Eastry's task was rather to ward off from his community the consequences of a respectful following of the archbishop's lead in opposition to the king and in firm adherence to the demands of Boniface VIII as set out in the bull *Clericis laicos*. In the event, Christ Church, faced with a crisis similar to, but far less desperate than, that of 1207, capitulated to the king, but Eastry guarded Winchelsey's interests and acted for a time as his vicar-general.

The weaker Walter Reynolds found in the prior an experienced and wary counsellor, firmly seated in the saddle and with advice to spare for others; consequently the archbishop turned often to him for guidance. This Eastry gave without stint: it was counsel of a piece with his character—cautious, realist, eminently level-headed. Himself unmoved by any personal or ideal considerations regarding the political and constitutional issues at stake in the last months of the reign of Edward II, he kept Reynolds trimming as best he could in awkward times, and would seem to have influenced a minor historical event by suggesting the representative deputation from parliament which urged the king's abdication at Kenilworth. Though lavish of advice Eastry was fearful of publicity, and several of his letters contain cryptic datings, instructions as to silence or requests for the destruction of what he had written. It must therefore have been supremely distasteful to him to learn that one of these private letters had been left lying for all to read, by some ironical accident, in the church of his native village.

With Mepeham, Reynolds's successor, Eastry, now perhaps an octogenarian, adopted a still more peremptory tone, and the archbishop on more than one occasion found himself the recipient of a 'snub from old Eastry', who did not hesitate to take the primate to task for his style of writing to his monks, and to outline the qualities desirable in the archbishop's officials.

Henry of Eastry's priorate was, in its domestic relations, one of the most peaceful Christ Church had known. The prior's efficiency, which never degenerated into fractious self-assertion or selfish domineering, commanded the respect of his community, and there is a welcome absence of the party warfare that so often marred the internal harmony of the house. What domestic troubles there were owed their existence to the aberrations of a few individuals and the misdemeanour of a clique of *mauvais sujets* who were responsible for a theft of plate and a libellous missive, and who clearly deserved the punishment that was late in coming. All other indications go to show that the prior, though a firm disciplinarian, was no ascetic or reformer, and rode his community on the snaffle in all matters of diet and old custom.

Eastry, like other great monastic superiors, was responsible for a number of additions to the treasure-chests and vestment-presses of the priory, and during his period of office, and presumably owing to his financial reorganization, the existing stone screen was erected round the monastic choir, together with a number of buildings in the precinct. Though he had been of university age when Thomism entered upon its victorious career, and though he had seen at close quarters the controversies of Kilwardby and Pecham, he evinces no direct interest in theology. He was, however, a patron of monk scholars, and a sheaf of letters has been preserved written to him by a group of young clerics connected in one way or another with Canterbury to whom he acted as patron in their university careers at Orleans, Bologna and elsewhere. It is interesting to see that these young men regarded him as a by no means inexorable friend and benefactor; it is also, perhaps, characteristic that their letters to the prior are, almost without exception, primarily concerned with money, and not at all with theology. When a direct request for advice on a theological point reached him, perhaps from the archbishop, it was at once passed on to the University of Oxford for a reply.[1]

Of spiritual or even of religious feeling there is no trace in the Eastry letters that have survived, and only too rarely does any touch of personal feeling escape the writer. He was a cool observer, not lightly to be stampeded. He had no great fears of invasion in 1325: the French, he said, would shake their fists at a man, but were slow to get their swords out of the scabbard; if they are scratched, they think all is over with them. His security, however, was not derived from any patriotic illusions: the men of Kent, he said, were a poor lot; if a hostile fleet appeared they would take to the woods and leave the fore-shore to others. He himself forestalled false alarms with a proclamation forbidding horns and trumpets to be blown in inland towns before the warning came from the coast.

Eastry, though blessed with a constitution which took him far beyond the common span of longevity, did not enjoy robust health, and there are many references in the letters to

[1] The question at issue was the Immaculate Conception.

illness and doctors. There is even one, to the physician himself, in which he reports progress and jests a little ponderously, and then thinks better of it and cancels the passage. He consulted a London specialist, leaving the local practitioner to his monks. In 1321 he felt his end was near, and drew up for the benefit of posterity an account of his economic achievements. He survived, however, for ten years more, and is found ordering from Flanders a little easy mule—not a great tall beast—on which he might amble down the familiar tracks and note with those keen eyes which now, perhaps, saw less clearly, how thick the stalks clustered and how full were the ears.

Registers, memoranda, letters, all were kept, and almost all have survived the chances of time and the carelessness of man, but there are no intimate sheets in the Eastry files. The old prior was not a *littérateur*, nor was he, we may guess, one who received or gave affection readily or who passed through the darkness and light of a spiritual progress. It was given to him to rule Christ Church for a longer span than any other prior between the Conquest and the Dissolution; a young man when Albert the Great, Thomas Aquinas and Bonaventure were in their prime, he lived into the age of Ockham and Marsilio; he saw the papacy attain its highest flight, and lived on to the days of Avignon. While he developed his estates and organized his finances, Dante, in a world of intenser passions, found time to watch the fireflies in the vineyards of Fiesole and mark the dewdrops on the hillside grass in the starlit dawn, while Giotto was rendering imperishable the daisies and pencilled elms of Umbria. To Eastry, the primroses of the Kentish brookland, the harebells and ragwort of the downs, the whispering reeds and dazzling levels of Thanet were familiar sights, but of such things he does not speak, and perhaps did not think. He saw the pastures with the eyes of Shallow, not with those of Perdita; his thoughts worked the

121

round of market prices, of stones of cheese, of bushels per acre, of the income from agistry, of the quality of the season's clip of wool. Stiff, dry and masterful, a great high farmer and superbly able man of business, he passes before us as he rides about the manors or sits at the chequer. He died, still active, while assisting at Mass, in April 1331.

XVII

THOMAS DE LA MARE

Thomas de la Mare (1309–96), a man with high family connections, was abbot of St Albans, the premier abbey of England, for about fifty years (1349–96); he was thus the contemporary of Wyclif, Langland and Chaucer and was in many respects both the greatest and the last of the abbots of the age of monastic magnificence.

THE long-lived abbot of St Albans, Thomas de la Mare, who held office for almost half a century and whom a distinguished modern historian, C. L. Kingsford, has named the greatest in the long line of abbots of the premier house of England, might well be considered the best representative of his century in the monastic world. Certainly it will not be disputed that Abbot de la Mare displays, magnified as it were to several dimensions, the qualities to be found in numerous prelates of his age; he occupies, in fact, very much the same place in monastic history as does Samson of Bury two centuries earlier, and had he found, like Samson, a *vates sacer* with a memory and a *naïveté* rivalling those of Jocelin of Brakelond, his name would doubtless be as familiar to his countrymen today.

His two predecessors had been men of marked individuality, if no more, and had shown, each in his own way, how such a house as St Albans could foster and give expansion to talents of all kinds that might otherwise have failed to blossom. Richard of Wallingford (*b.* 1291), the son of a blacksmith, was adopted, no doubt on account of his manifest promise, by the then prior of Wallingford, who sent him to Oxford—the Oxford of Duns Scotus—where he passed successfully through the arts course, and at the age of twenty-three asked for the monastic habit at St Albans. This no doubt fulfilled the hopes, amounting almost to a tacit bargain, which had inspired Prior William Kirkby's original patronage. After only three years of monastic life he was back at Oxford, this time at Gloucester College, to study theology. In after years he lamented his short abode in the cloister, as also an excessive addiction, while at Oxford, to the mathematical studies for which the university of Grosseteste and Roger Bacon was famous, and which included both astronomy and astrology. Becoming a Bachelor in 1326, he returned to St Albans, to ask for the festive expenses of his inauguration, just in time to be present at the death of Abbot Hugh of Eversdene. Richard was clearly the most brilliant of the coming generation at St Albans, for he was chosen as preacher on election day and as one of the nine to whom the election was compromised. We are told that at Mass that morning he had resolved to accept as from God the result of the day's debate and when, after long discussion, the choice of his fellow-electors fell on him, he accepted the omen. Unlike his immediate predecessors he lived simply as abbot, dispensing with servants and companions and customary presents, and having with him only a single chaplain, while at the solemn feast on his reception at the abbey on returning from Rome he dined with the brethren, leaving the magnates to dine by themselves in the abbatial hall.

Like other abbots of St Albans, he revised the constitutions of the house, and made decrees for Redburn, the holiday resort of the monks. He also drew up a list of the decrees of the provincial chapter, while continuing his own astronomical and geometrical studies. Among his additions to the abbey were the new mechanical clock and the almonry school with its offices, and the private chapel in his lodging, with its adornments. His biographer notes, in the fashion that Matthew Paris had set in the *Gesta Abbatum*, that many thought he would have been better advised to pay off some of the debts of his predecessor before making any of his own. What might have been a distinguished reign was, however, shadowed from the first and prematurely ended by a long illness, diagnosed as leprosy, which attacked his sight and later his voice and rendered him all but impotent in the last few years of his life; from 1333 he had his prior as coadjutor. He died in May 1335.

His successor was, like himself, a scholar, and the type throughout the ages made a peculiar appeal to the electors of St Albans. Born of parents of easy circumstances, he was sent by them to Oxford, and took his mastership in arts. Then Michael of Mentmore, like Richard of Wallingford before him, took the habit and in due course returned to Oxford, where he proceeded bachelor in divinity. He was apparently still at Oxford when Abbot Richard died, and was chosen to succeed him ten days later.

Abbot Michael was an indulgent patron of scholars, re-arranging the time-table in their favour and building out of his own revenues a group of studies between the dorter and the chapel of the guesthouse, so that they might not suffer the disturbances of the cloister. He continued to take part in the monastic affairs of the province, and was elected president for the whole of his reign save for an interval of three years; he was also sufficiently in favour with the young Edward III to be asked to stand god-father to his youngest son, Edmund of Langley, the future Duke of York. Premature death, however, took him away; he was one of the first to die when the Black Death struck St Albans; taken ill on Maundy Thursday, he died on Easter Day.

Thomas de la Mare, in contrast to his predecessors, was of distinguished family, with forebears who had taken their part in public life, and with connections among the baronial houses such as the Montagues, the de la Zouches and the Grandissons. Sir Peter de la Mare, Speaker of the Parliament of 1376, was probably a relative. Strikingly handsome both as boy and as man, he had the refined features, the long, thin hands and the pure complexion that observers noted in more than one of the outstanding men of that age, and which have been perpetuated in the effigies of Gloucester and Westminster, and in the Wilton diptych. Educated in letters by his parents, he never passed through the schools of Oxford; though highly intelligent, he had not a scholar's or a theologian's mind, but as a young monk he studied composition, and later, when prior of Tynemouth, he became expert in the current fashion of preaching both in English and Latin with the help of some Austin friars, and in particular of John Waldeby, later provincial, who dedicated to him a series of homilies which he had written at the prior's request.

Attracted from youth to things religious and to the liturgy of the Church, he resolved to become a monk, apparently at the early age of seventeen. He was one of a large family, and three brothers and a sister followed his example; of his brothers one came to St Albans, one went to the Cluniac house of Thetford, and a third became a canon, and ultimately abbot, of Missenden; the sister took the veil at the nunnery of Delapré, near her brother's abbey. The vocations of the family are an interesting indication that aristocratic recruits still found their way to the most varied homes. It is equally interesting to learn that an aspirant of such high rank and promise should have been sent to pass his noviciate at a distance from St Albans at the dependency of Wymondham. There he remained till the death of Abbot Richard in 1335, when Abbot Michael recalled him to fill in rapid succession the posts of abbot's chaplain, kitchener, cellarer and lastly prior of Tynemouth. There his prudent administration, his social gifts and his zeal for observance gained him a name in the north among nobility and common people; he also gave evidence of his readiness— never wanting throughout his long life—to vindicate in the courts on behalf of his house any claim that he regarded as just.

He had been nine years at Tynemouth when the first visitation of the Black Death carried off Abbot Michael on Easter Sunday, 1349. More than fifty of the monks died with him, including prior and subprior, and this may have smoothed the way for de la Mare's candidature. Even so, he was apparently not the first choice of the electors to whom the convent had delegated powers, but when the prior of Wymondham refused to take office Thomas was chosen. He was about forty years old.

As abbot, he speedily made a name for himself. Edward III made him a Privy Councillor and remained on friendly terms, though with intervals of misunderstanding. The Black Prince was a closer friend, to whom the older man acted as counsellor and confidant; the Prince became a confrater of the abbey, and on at least one occasion defended the abbot with filial piety. A third distinguished friend was the captured King John of France, who spent some time at St Albans. The close friendship with the Black Prince, and the sympathies of a St Albans chronicler with the abbot's namesake (or relation), the Speaker of the Good Parliament of 1376, suggests that de la Mare's interest lay with the opposition in the later decades of the old king's reign, but of this the abbey chronicler says nothing.

In monastic affairs, Abbot Thomas succeeded on election to the office of first president of the black monks, held by the late Abbot de Mentmore, and three years later he was elected to the post in his own right. He remained president, with or without a coadjutor, for twenty years, and fulfilled his duties with energy. In addition to framing two sets of statutes for the province, he drew up minute constitutions for his own house and its dependencies, giving especial attention to the devout performance of the liturgy, prescribing a slower recitation and some added chant, while at the same time pruning off excrescences of vocal prayer. His position and reputation combined to make him the outstanding abbot of his day, and the king employed him to visit the monasteries of Eynsham, Abingdon, Battle and Reading, where various degrees of royal patronage existed, and he performed the same duties elsewhere, as at Chester and Bury. It may be remarked that the only charges of extravagance made against him were in connection with his expenses as president; it is also perhaps characteristic that he was the most energetic collector of funds on behalf of Richard Fitzralph during his controversy with the friars.

Extravagant or not, de la Mare was certainly in his years of health an abbot in the grand style. In parliament he asserted his right of precedence before all other abbots. He was a tireless litigant against great and small, ecclesiastical and lay, local and remote adversaries, and was almost as often a defendant; besides the innumerable miscellaneous suits on which he embarked or into which he was drawn, he contributed his page to the time-honoured controversies with the bishops of Lincoln and Norwich concerning exemption, and with the townspeople of St Albans regarding their liberties. Though often victorious, he had his reverses, and shared in the calamities of the times. If the first visitation of the plague had put him into power the second, which struck him down, left him with a painful legacy of disease and in his old age he was disturbed, and forced for a time to capitulate, by the rising of 1381 in which the inhabitants of St Albans exploited their private grievances. A man of practical rather than speculative intelligence, he took no direct interest, so far as can be seen, in the new and vital controversies that were sapping the foundations of his world; his support of Fitzralph was probably an act of the president's *esprit de corps*, and in the polemics between Wyclif and the possessioners, and in the later Lollard controversies, he appears only as a cautious counsellor.

De la Mare was a munificent superior and a magnificent builder. The great gateway, the washing-place in the cloister, the King's Hall and the New Chamber for distinguished guests were probably his most memorable undertakings, but his hand was present everywhere repairing, furnishing, rebuilding and enlarging in the airy, more comfortable manner of domestic planning that was becoming the fashion. The cloister was glazed and furnished with seats, a room was fitted up for his chaplains and studies for the Oxford scholars, a set of apartments was constructed with ornamental ceilings and a decoration of shields and stars in gold and green; furniture of all kinds, silver-plate, chests and books added wealth and beauty to the cluster of buildings where the new cream ashlar met the warm red of the Roman tiles. Nor were sacristy and church forgotten; vestments, vessels, service-books, lamps, hangings and pictures poured in, and among the last was one brought at great expense from north Italy; not the least costly item (which formed a less justifiable article in the charge of extravagance) was a great clock of the kind now coming into fashion. De la Mare's personal taste in things rich and beautiful appears in the gift of a silver-gilt eagle with wings outspread to stand on the crest of the shrine of St Alban, and in the provision, during his lifetime, of a marble tomb and elaborate brasses for his predecessor, Abbot Michael, and himself. When the reader of the long catalogue pauses to form a picture of the roofs and pillars and windows and panelling of the vast group of buildings, of the shimmer of silks and velvet,

the lustre of precious metal, and the glow of lamps on cande-
labra and jewels, he can well understand that Thomas de la
Mare was prepared to contribute generously to any collection
taken up on behalf of the protagonist of the *possessionati*; he
can understand also something of the grievances of the towns-
folk in 1381 and of the members of the parliament of 1410
who suggested that the religious houses should be nationalized
to provide funds for foreign wars and social services at home.
Whatever value we may set upon the objects of the abbot's
benefactions, and however great their intrinsic beauty, the
funds came for the most part neither from spontaneous
offerings nor from payment for work done or services
rendered by his monks, but from the labour of peasants on the
abbey estates and from those burdened in various shapes and
forms with the charges of the abbey's churches.

Yet if we compare de la Mare with the great ecclesiastical
patrons of a century and a half later—with Cardinal Wolsey
and Cardinal d'Amboise, to say nothing of the Medici and
Colonna and d'Este—the man and his works stand in strong
contrast. In the abbot's expenses there was no directly
personal luxury and little personal display; his gifts adorned
the abbey church or added to the amenities of the monastery;
they did not primarily cater for the pride of life; they were for
the enjoyment of many and would, had the fates been more
kind, have remained for the eyes of posterity till they crumbled.
The man himself stands in still stronger contrast. It comes,
perhaps, as a surprise to those who have read widely in the
sources of monastic history of the fourteenth century to find
how practical was the devotion and how ascetic the life of
Thomas de la Mare. Here he could have learnt little from
Samson or the most observant of the Anglo-Norman monks.
He rose before midnight, from a bed penitential in its rough-
ness, while the community still slept, and recited his private

Office or lengthy prayers; after celebrating Mass he heard three or four more. He let no occupation, however absorbing, no visitor, however distinguished, stand in the way of his punctual observance of the Hours, and when he had a spare half-hour in his room or on a journey, he recited the Penitential Psalms or the Office of the Dead, as had Wulfstan of Worcester almost three centuries before. He seldom ate or drank more than once in the day, and practised fixed fasts and abstinences in addition to those of the Church and monastic custom; he wore a hair-shirt and received the discipline at the hands of another every week; he observed strictly the times and places of monastic silence. Though as a boy he had known and enjoyed as an expert the field sports of his class, he refused as a monk to take part even as a spectator in hunting or hawking, nor would he allow those under his rule to do so. Yet if rigid himself, he was an excellent host, studious of the comfort of others and with the easy urbanity of a man of breeding.

Though we possess a long and detailed account of his administration and his lawsuits there are few of the intimate details, domestic incidents and revealing snatches of conversation that enable us to catch glimpses of the living Samson or Ailred, nor do any personal letters remain. It is therefore not possible to judge how far de la Mare's austere rule of life was the reflection of a character that was by nature serious, determined and energetic, or whether he gave also an impression of a deeper spirituality drawing its strength from a hidden source. We may perhaps be allowed to feel that the ultimate touch of holiness is wanting, and that de la Mare was neither a Wulfstan nor an Anselm. He ruled, however, with love, never happier than when among his monks, whose voices in the liturgy delighted him above all other melody. He often stayed at Redburn with the monks in *villeggiatura*, ringing the bells for office when others failed to do so,[1] and smilingly putting a forfeit of wine on latecomers to dinner. On a deeper level, the chronicler tells us of a service of the sick which is in the true line of Christian and monastic charity; he visited and consoled them, and did not hesitate to perform the most menial services or to give the most delicate marks of affection. It is pleasant to learn that in his own long-drawn decay he received a willing return. His wishes were gladly met when he desired, between Compline at night and Mass of the next day—the monastic greater silence—to be served by none save his own monks; he preferred their services freely given, he said, to those of any others, however skilled.

Attacked by the plague at its second visitation (no doubt that of 1361–2) he never shook off its legacy of infection and disease, but he long continued the ascetic practices of his vigorous manhood; he bore his growing infirmities with dignity and refused to interrupt the tenor of his life and its occupations until extreme old age sapped his physical and mental powers. It should, however, be remembered that he made a genuine attempt to resign his office, but was prevented by the instance of the Black Prince and the remonstrances of his monks. He remained abbot, therefore, until his death, but for the last nine years he was a complete invalid, suffering from a complication of painful maladies which ultimately rendered him helpless in body and weakened in mind, though he retained full consciousness. Throughout these trying years he was nursed assiduously by his monks—'in motherly wise',

[1] It may be perhaps permissible, as showing how human nature remains the same now as in the fourteenth century, to quote some words written of a modern abbot, Dom Cuthbert Butler of Downside (1858–1934): 'Many years ago a certain junior monk, when "antiphoner", omitted to ring the prescribed bells. Abbot Butler often supplied the defect. One day he left in the junior's room a note to this effect: "Shall be away to-day. Please get another to ring Angelus. E.C.B."' (*Memoir* in *Downside Review*, XXXIII (1934), 430.)

the chronicler records, adding that no son could have watched over his father, no wife over her husband, with more patience. Failing slowly, he died on the octave of the Nativity of Our Lady, 15 September 1396, aged eighty-seven; seventy-one years had been spent in the habit and forty-seven as abbot. He had led, in a certain sense, a double life. That of the great prelate was open for all to see; of the other how much, we may wonder, did the eyes of a Wyclif, a Langland or a Chaucer perceive, when they fell upon the abbot of St Albans riding from London to Westminster to take precedence of all the abbots of England? Did they know of the hair-shirt, the vigils and the fasting? We cannot say, nor do we ourselves know how many of the abbots of England, in an age when the medieval world and its faiths were crumbling, lived as devoutly and as austerely. We can, however, well say that had many thus lived in the days of Henry VIII their order would not have passed, and would not have deserved to pass, so easily from the English scene.

XVIII

UTHRED OF BOLDON

Uthred of Boldon (? 1315–96), was monk and subprior of Durham cathedral priory, which at that time had an intellectual and economic pre-eminence among the monasteries of northern England. The opponent of Wyclif, he was nevertheless accused of unorthodoxy as a 'nominalist', but remained a respected and influential figure. He spent much of his life as prior of Durham College (now Trinity College) at Oxford, and was the most celebrated 'university monk' of his age.

JOHN UTHRED never held office as superior of a great monastery; he may nevertheless not inaptly be regarded as the most eminent English monk of his time after the abbot of St Albans, while he is certainly the only monk from north of the Humber to win a high reputation in the south during the century. He is, besides, a principal ornament of a house that inherited a long tradition of fine culture. John Uthred, called of Boldon, may indeed stand as the representative monk-scholar of his age, the century's typical figure in the long series that stretches in England from Bede to Aelfric, William of Malmesbury and Matthew Paris, and is taken up later in France by Luc D'Achery and Jean Mabillon, to be continued in our own day by Dom Ursmer Berlière, Dom André Wilmart, Dom Germain Morin and Dom Jean Leclercq.

John Uthred, a northerner, if not a Scot, by birth, probably spent much of his childhood on the coastal flats between the estuaries of Wear and Tyne; his home, with its distinctive, far-seen church, lay almost exactly midway between the two monastic settlements of Jarrow and Wearmouth hallowed by memories of Bede and Benet Biscop. The manor from which he took his name belonged to Durham, and it may have been there that the bursar or some other official on his rounds heard of the promising boy. He did not, however, go to Durham for his schooling, and when, at the age of thirteen or so, he began his arts course at Oxford it was as a secular student. The course was interrupted by his decision to become a monk; he was professed at Durham in 1342 and five years later returned to Oxford after three years at the Durham cell of Stamford. Oxford was his home for twenty years; he took his doctorate in 1357, a little before Fitzralph's final onslaught on the friars, and almost fifteen years before Wyclif left philosophy for divinity.

Uthred's working life, so far as it is visible, falls into two periods, though some of his interests and activities were common to both. There is the continuous residence of twenty years at Oxford (1347–67) during part of which he was regent master, and during the whole of which he was occupied with academic questions, and became involved in a series of academic controversies; and there is the later period of thirty years (1367–96) during the whole of which, save for a short interlude at Oxford (1383–6), he was in office either at Durham or the neighbouring Finchale, and was occupied principally in monastic and other ecclesiastical business.

Uthred soon became one of the most distinguished teachers at Oxford. Had we only his historical and monastic treatises by which to judge him, we might picture him as a venerable and peace-loving student. In fact, he took a leading part in the controversies of his day, showing something of the pugnacity and partisan zeal that was to become so familiar under Wyclif, and as regent proposed a number of theological opinions (which he defended with acerbity) that were both novel and rash.

His first excursion into polemics seems to have been during

the last phase of the great controversy on evangelical poverty and the mendicant ideal which had recently been given a practical turn by Archbishop Fitzralph. Uthred was the author of at least two tracts against mendicancy, and it was this, no doubt, that ranged the friars against him and ultimately led to his academic undoing. When (*c.* 1365) the friars turned their apologetics into a frontal attack upon the property-owning clerks and religious, and even gave support to the demand for some sort of confiscation, Uthred came forward as the protagonist of his order and the author of two treatises on the superiority of the spiritual over the temporal power and on the lawfulness of church endowment, and determined against Wyclif on these matters. In this he once more attacked the Minors' interpretation of evangelical poverty, and added for full measure a sharp rebuke to the false brethren attacking their Mother's dower. However well deserved his attack may have been—and his arguments in general are sane and persuasive—he could not have expected it to act as an emollient.

Meanwhile Uthred had, with the majority of his contemporaries, chosen his theological opinions from many schools, including that of the Ockhamists, while his views on grace resembled those of the doctors stigmatized by Bradwardine a few years previously as 'Pelagian'. This by itself, however, would probably not have brought him to grief. He had, however, excogitated a particular opinion to which he was firmly wedded, and which he applied to a whole series of problems; this was the thesis of the *clara visio*, the vision of some aspect of divine truth granted to all between apparent and real death, carrying with it the fateful choice or rejection of God upon which depended the eternal salvation or shipwreck of the soul. This in the fullness of time was attacked by the Friars Preachers and delated to the archbishop of Canterbury;

Uthred fought back with spirit, and his vituperation must have supplied any stimulus that was still wanting to his opponents; after a solemn examination by a panel of theologians the majority of the propositions were censured by Archbishop Langham and declared inadmissible in public teaching at Oxford.

No contemporary account of the affair exists, but it is at least remarkable that at the very crisis of the episode Uthred was recalled to be prior of Finchale, a small dependency of Durham within easy reach of the priory, which was used as a rest-house by monks in *villeggiatura*. His confrères clearly did not regard the episode as a disgrace; they may even have regarded Uthred as something of a martyr at the hands of the mendicants, but his prestige and self-confidence as a speculative theologian must have been shaken, and while it would be false to regard Uthred as a fourteenth-century Loisy or Fénelon, or to think of the censure as comparable with the condemnation of Wyclif a few years later, yet the blow must have been a sensible one, and may well have played its part in bringing to an end the era of free academic speculation at Oxford.

For the next fifteen years Uthred passed in rotation from the post of prior at Finchale (1367–8, 1375–81) to that of subprior at Durham (1368–75, 1381–3) and we can trace his activities in the former office both in the accounts which he presented to the mother house, and in the record of expenses incurred by him on various journeys. Already from early days at Oxford he was a well-known figure among the black monks, and from 1360 onwards for a series of years he represented his house at chapter; in 1363 he was one of the committee of diffinitors who considered the new statutes of de la Mare, and in 1366 he was delegated to visit the troublesome abbey of Whitby, the scene of recent scandals, and together with the abbot of St Mary's, York, to report on the success of the recent disciplinary measures. Such commissions, given to a man of forty who had held no high office, are evidence of the reputation for sound judgment and tactful dealing acquired by Uthred among his brethren. His fame, indeed, had spread outside his order in circles which would have taken little heed of Langham's censure, and he was generally regarded as the representative spokesman of the monastic body in the country. This is shown in a striking manner in a chronicle which under the year 1371 introduces four regular theologians to be questioned by the Black Prince at a royal council as to the degree of jurisdiction enjoyed by the pope in temporal matters; side by side with Uthred on the bench were the provincials of the Minors and the Preachers. The probability that the passage is a tendentious exaggeration or even an entirely fictitious squib does not diminish its significance for Uthred's reputation, and it is not surprising to find that in 1373 he should in actual fact have been chosen one of the small embassy sent by the king to Avignon to negotiate on a question of papal subsidy. Here again the appointment of a monk who was not a prelate is probably without parallel in the century. His engagement in ecclesiastical affairs continued, and casual notes in account books show him to have been at York for convocation in 1370–1; as visitor of the churches of Howdenshire in 1379–80, and again in 1383–4; and as visitor of the northern monasteries as delegate of the chapter in 1380–1. He was one of the trustees of the fund left by Bishop Hatfield for the endowment of Durham College, and travelled to London and Oxford on business connected with this. He took no direct part in the various moves and councils issuing in the condemnation of Wyclif, but it is probably to the later part of his career that belong two treatises in which he defended traditional doctrine on two burning questions of the day, the Eucharist and Predestination. To this period, perhaps, belong also his apologetics of the monastic way of life as against the friars, who were urging their claims to superiority on the score both of their poverty and of their greater antiquity. On the last point something of a *mêlée* was in progress in which all the orders were engaged; the Augustinians of every description claiming unbroken descent from their patron, while the Carmelites, by tracing their pedigree back to the prophet Elias, successfully outbid all the regulars save for a small group of Preachers who had the enterprising courage to rely on their popular title in staking out a claim upon the patriarch Jacob as their founder.[1] To the literature of this controversy Uthred contributed several writings of greater solidity and worth than the topic might have seemed to promise. One of these, a revised version of a treatise on monastic origins, became an extremely reasonable, persuasive and historically accurate account of the development of the monastic ideal, as seen first in kindred endeavours in the Old Testament and by St John the Baptist, and traced from apostolic times through Cassian and the monks of Palestine to the Italian monks of the age of St Benedict. This treatise had as complement one on the essence of the monastic life, perhaps composed as a manual for novice-masters, which again with extreme reasonableness, if also with some quaint touches and topical references, showed that the monastic life was in effect the perfect Christian life; that it was, in fact, that lived by our first parents in Paradise.

Uthred was again in Oxford for three years from 1383. It was the year after the solemn condemnation of Wyclif, and the academic climate had changed greatly since the days of Uthred's inception. Wyclif had gone, and was pouring forth

---

[1] The Preachers were known in France and England as *Jacobitae* from their Paris convent of St James.

a molten flood of pamphlets from Lutterworth; the university had been roughly handled by Courtenay, and the friars and monks of all orders had drawn together to defend the Eucharist and resist the attacks of the followers of Wyclif, the first generation of Lollards, on the religious life and on the whole framework of the Church as they knew it. What Uthred thought or did in this new world we do not know; he may have returned merely in order to set the newly organized college on its feet. He returned to be prior of Finchale for the third time in 1386, and there, ten years later, he died. To his last years belongs, perhaps, the group of devotional writings and notices of monastic saints and writers that are still extant.

Uthred is in large part hidden from us by that veil which covers so many of the distinguished thinkers of his century, from Marsilio to Wyclif, and which baffles all search for personality and intimacy. His writings hold no allusions to his own life; they are formal in construction and often depend so largely on previous work that it is impossible to separate his own contribution. His theological opinions, as known to us from his tract, are of interest chiefly as showing the lack of any fixed tradition in the Oxford of his day, but they show also an independent mind, at grips with real problems, not merely a technician in theological gymnastic. His reputation was very high; it is not possible to recall another black monk beneath the rank of abbot who held a position in the age at all comparable to his; that his memory was held in honour at Durham is shown by the care taken, forty years after his death and possibly by Prior Wessington, to assemble a series of dates covering the changes of residence and office in his life. Yet only one saying, 'that the accidents should never be preferred to the substance' by the student, remains to reveal his character. He wrote and thought in the academic idiom of his day, and this, though it may have advanced his fame among his contemporaries, rendered his work sterile; the future, the distant future, lay with the hidden, spontaneous writers of English, with Rolle, with Langland, with the unknown authors of *The Cloud of Unknowing* and *Pearl*. Uthred lived to see the age of Chaucer and Piers Plowman, but there is nothing in his work that speaks of it. Laborious, sane and often convincing in his argument, he had neither the fresh outlook on his own world nor the resources for a critical survey of the past which both before his time and after have given to the work of monastic scholars a permanent value for the ages. His adult life was divided almost equally between the routine of a teacher at Oxford, the liturgical and social round of community life in its most dignified form at Durham, and the quieter, simpler days in the shady valley by the Wear with its old memories of Godric and its present succession of brethren taking their rest and refreshment by the pleasant waters. Through all this he passes, a figure to us dignified and not unsympathetic, whom few of today's visitors recall as they walk over the fields from Durham along the path that must have been so familiar to his eyes, and stand on the grass *ante introitum chori* beneath which his bones are lying.

XIX

JOHN WYCLIF

John Wyclif (? 1330–82) a Yorkshireman, became a well-known master of arts at Oxford, at Merton, Balliol (where he was Master), Canterbury (where he was Warden for a short time) and Queen's colleges, and began his career as teacher and writer in 1360. Some twenty years later he incepted in theology and his doctrine on the Eucharist was regarded as unorthodox. After a first inconclusive trial for heresy he devoted his energies to a general attack on the pope, the hierarchy, the sacramental system, the religious orders, the doctrine of transubstantiation and other current beliefs, and became the inspirer of a group of itinerant preachers, with a simple gospel message, who were the predecessors and heralds of the Lollards. Though finally censured by the archbishop of Canterbury and forced to leave Oxford, he was never formally excommunicated and died at his benefice of Lutterworth (Leicestershire).

PROBABLY no character in English history has suffered such distortion at the hands of friend and foe as has that of John Wyclif. While no historian has yet been able to approach him with perfect sobriety of judgment, the events of his career, the authenticity of many of the works attributed to him, the degree of his speculative powers, and even the spelling of his name, have been, and still are, matters of controversy. Here it is not necessary to enter into any of these discussions, as the main lines of his charges against the religious can be seen clearly enough in works which are certainly genuine.

The views of Wyclif upon the religious life and its contemporary practitioners underwent, as did his views on almost every aspect of religion, a considerable modification in the last fifteen years of his life. His adversaries, writing years after, attributed his hostility to the monks to his unfortunate experiences at Canterbury College, from the mastership of which he had been expelled by Simon Langham, whose action had been upheld on appeal by the pope. It may well have been so: but his attitude to the possessioners was the logical outcome both of his early sympathy with the Spiritual friars, his later theories of grace and dominion, and his alliance with the opposition to Rome, and it harmonized with all the other developments of his thought at this time. In any case, the rift had occurred by 1374, and henceforward the monks, as one of the 'sects', are contrasted with the followers of the pure doctrine of Christ, though they are attacked far less violently than the Roman Curia on the one hand and the four orders of friars on the other. They err in following the Rule of Benedict rather than that of Christ, and like all possessioners they depart from the Master's ideal and their own profession by enjoying secular rents and still more by appropriating the funds of parish churches. They are, moreover, notoriously well found in every kind of cattle and provisions, which they squander and waste beyond all other men with intolerable carelessness. Such accusations are made more than once, but despite the wide and exposed target presented by the monks, Wyclif devotes singularly little space to accusations against them. He had, however, once and for all broken with them in his reply to Uthred and Binham; in this, his first piece of publicist writing, the *Determinacio*, he argued that goods bestowed for spiritual uses should, if not used according to this purpose, be restored to their donors, and that in default of action on the part of the spiritual authorities, the heirs of the original donors might resume possession. Such arguments, though calculated to rouse hostility to their author among the older orders, were calm and academic in comparison with those directed against the friars.

Yet with these, also, the relations of Wyclif had not always been unfriendly. There is no record of any serious quarrel during the first twenty-five years of his residence at Oxford; he had translated the Rule and Testament of St Francis, and when warden of Canterbury College is said to have worn a rough gown similar to that of the Minors. In later years he had the support of the friars—or at least of the Minors and Austin friars—in his early opposition to papal demands and to clerical dominion, and there is an interesting record of a friendly interchange of lecture notes between him and William Wodeford, a leading Minorite doctor at Oxford, as late as *c.* 1370. Even when the break occurred he did not feel it useless to issue a last appeal to those of the friars who had fought with him in the past. When, however, he openly rejected transubstantiation and broke with the papacy, he drew upon himself opposition from all the four orders, in particular the Minors and the Carmelites, while he himself, with ever-increasing bitterness of feeling, launched a series of counter-attacks which far surpassed in virulence any assaults of which he had been the object.

In these treatises and pamphlets, which issued from the rectory of Lutterworth in journalistic profusion during the last three years of his life, Wyclif abused the religious of England, monks, canons and friars, through all the moods and tenses. Not since the days of Gerald of Wales had any body of men received such a drenching. There is, indeed, a certain superficial similarity between the writings of the two men. With both, the mention of their *bête noire* released an inexhaustible stream of words; neither writer achieved or even aimed at economy or compression, and both were prepared to repeat the same charges and arguments and turns of phrase *usque ad nauseam*; with both there is a note of personal anger, and in both the fixed idea is betrayed by the tireless iteration. There, however, the resemblance ends. There is between the two an essential difference of aim and method. While Gerald's purpose, so far as he had one consciously in mind, was to mend monasticism, Wyclif desired nothing but to end it. Gerald's normal method was to support a series of sweeping general charges with a limited number of examples drawn from his own experience; Wyclif devoted his energies to demolishing the whole system by *a priori* reasoning based on Scriptural, theological and historical considerations. Finally, while Gerald retained a sympathy with the ideals of monasticism and a fond memory of individuals from the golden past, Wyclif, in the impersonal manner that distinguishes all his writing and that seems to reflect a mind to which personal affection was a stranger, omits all mention of the misdeeds of individuals, as he omits also any reference to the more amiable qualities of those who had once been his friends.

The pamphlets directed against the friars belong, as has been mentioned, without exception to the last few years of Wyclif's life and principally to the period when, exiled from Oxford, he had seen his teaching publicly condemned and his itinerant followers harassed and obstructed, and when, warned by a first stroke that his days were numbered and conscious at the same time of his teeming brain, he worked with feverish haste before the night should fall, with an embittered spirit and a mind, perhaps, pathologically obdurate and inflexible, to leave a mass of seed to be drawn upon and broadcast by his disciples after his death. This sour legacy of hatred, passed from mouth to mouth in England for a few years only, and then slumbering for centuries in the libraries of central Europe, has within the last seventy years been made public property for the first time. The reader who endures to pass through its parching expanse may indeed be repelled by the total lack of spiritual warmth, but he can scarcely fail to recognize the mental power and single-minded purpose with which it is animated.

Wyclif's central thesis is simple and radical enough. All organized bodies among the Christian community, all set forms of life and government, are 'sects', at best superfluous, at worst infernal, in any case opposed to the one true sect or way of life instituted by Christ. Four sects in particular stand condemned: the pope, together with his cardinals and prelates; the orders of monks; the orders of regular canons; and the four orders of friars. All receive summary judgment. The pope, whose claim to be the Vicar of Christ is inconceivably preposterous, is unsurpassed for open and shameless transgression of the Ten Commandments; he is not only mendacious, but is quintessential mendacity itself; he is the Antichrist *par excellence* of the Western World; the monks, long since unfaithful to whatever good there may have been in their Rule, have absorbed so much land and wealth that all the poor of England could live on the rent; the canons' relationship to the father of lies is sufficiently shown by their claim to have Augustine for their founder; and finally the friars, compact of lies from the sole of the foot to the crown of the head, have been launched upon the world in these latter days by the devil himself. The Scriptures, Wyclif urges, abound in types of these pests: the pope is Gog; the other three sects Magog. As for the four orders of friars, all children of Cain who slew his brother, they may be seen in figure in the four beasts of Daniel: the bear, the leopard and the lioness stand for the Preachers, the Minors and the Austin friars; the fourth beast, with its ten horns and its teeth and claws of iron, bears a remarkable resemblance to the Carmelites. All are apostates, idolaters, schismatics, heretics; their houses are strongholds of murder and rapine, Caim's castles;[1] it would be more tolerable

[1] 'Castella caimitica.' Wyclif relished the phrase and repeated it frequently, even if he did not originae it. Thinking that the correct spelling of the name of the first murderer was Caim he took the letters as initials of the Carmelites, Augustinians, Jacobites (i.e. Dominicans) and Minors.

for England to be ravaged by her enemies than to be secretly devoured by infidels of this kind; poisonous vermin as they are, they should be smoked out of their nests and destroyed with all their brood like rats or vipers. And Wyclif concludes with a verse from the liturgy in which all angels and saints are implored to drive the demons out of christendom.

Such passages, in which the most distinguished theologian of his generation at Oxford rails at the friars like a drab, abound in Wyclif's polemical works. They are an early and melancholy example of a type of literature that was to remain only too common throughout the religious controversies of succeeding centuries. Wyclif, however, had a mind capable of a higher flight than this, and if in the realm of mere abuse he helped to found a genre of English writing, he also laid down, with singular fullness of detail, the main lines along which all future attacks upon the religious moved.

With dogged insistence he beats home, throughout his tracts, a series of accusations against the friars that became commonplaces of all future controversy. There is, first, the charge that the mendicants, armed with special powers, using every blandishment, and appearing from time to time as birds of passage, were able to attract penitents away from the parish priest; the latter in consequence lost the knowledge of souls to which a pastor has a right, in addition to losing the gifts which a natural generosity might prompt or less worthy considerations extract. The penitent, for his part, having thus the opportunity of approaching a series of confessors personally unknown to him, lost the care of a single spiritual physician who might be supposed to understand his case, besides avoiding an occasion of natural shame which might act as a deterrent.

Next, the friars were accused of beguiling widows and young people, of living upon them and of cajoling them into parting with every kind of commodity. No bolt or bar was proof against a friar. Moreover, they used their privileged position at the university and elsewhere to induce boys of promise, or those who were heirs to property, to become friars; chicanery and even violence were employed when more straightforward methods failed. These accusations led naturally on to that of immorality, which Wyclif often makes by way of apophasis.[1] While the young friars intrigued with servant girls, the more experienced were accused of corrupting even ladies of noble blood. Finally, from the proceeds of begging and unscrupulous dealing of all kinds, the friars built magnificent churches, sumptuously decorated and furnished, and provided themselves with spacious and comfortable homes.

In addition to these and other charges, common to all critics of the age, there are two which recur, and are peculiar to Wyclif: the charge that the friars by begging and dispatching money abroad are ruining the realm, and that they are heretical on the subject of the Eucharist. To the first Wyclif returns several times, and with characteristic thoroughness supplies again and again calculations of the gross sum thus lost either by dispatch overseas or in the construction of Caim's castles. A conservative estimate, he says, puts the number of English friars at four thousand; if £5 a year be allowed for the keep of each and another £5 per head for building and other overhead costs, some £40,000 is taken from the wealth of England by drones every year; they do nothing in return but corrupt the gospel teaching.[2]

The charge of heresy against the friars was a necessary rejoinder to their attack on Wyclif. His polemics against them

[1] 'I will not mention', etc.
[2] The number 4000, which would have been roughly correct for 1348, should certainly be almost halved for 1380. There were at the time some 200 friaries in existence, but many of these must have been small houses with less than ten inmates, inclusive of lay brothers.

PLATE V

THOMAS DE LA MARE

PLATE VI

FINCHALE PRIORY

date without exception from the last years of his life, and undoubtedly owe their origin to the firm stand taken by them against his doctrine on the Eucharist. In response, he retorts the charge: the friars are heretical in their incomprehensible and novel teaching of transubstantiation; faithful to the pope and holding him for infallible, they maintain a preposterous theory of accidents remaining without substance, which they dare not put in plain English for ordinary Christians, but shuffle and evade the issue as to what is present in a consecrated Host.

These individual charges, however, are such as any critic might make. It is not these which make the assaults of Wyclif on the religious life something new and formidable. The capacity of his mind to penetrate the surface and touch the springs of life below, the unshrinking logic with which he draws conclusions from his accusations, the cold and drastic purpose behind his words, all of which were to bear fruit in due season, are more clearly seen in the frontal attack which he makes on the whole system, and the radical and unflinching campaign of extermination which he proposes. While others, before and after, were content to abuse the friars, Wyclif drives hard against their origins, ideals, pretensions and methods. While others were content to reform, Wyclif's hatred could be satisfied only with the complete extinction of his opponent. *Ecrasez l'infâme.* It is in this, and in his appeal to the alleged purity and utter simplicity of a primitive age, that his significance consists. By proceeding thus, he gave the go-by to all the elaborate framework of ethics and apologetics, to all the mass of speculation and tradition, that had gone to make the *Summa theologica*, and threw the *onus probandi* back upon those who for centuries had scarcely felt the need to expound their ideals, still less to defend them and prove their truth.

With a lucidity and precision which contrast strongly with the diffusion and apparent disorder of many of his treatises, Wyclif lays down the broad lines of attack which future generations did little more than develop. Originally, so his theory has it, clergy of the apostolic model had ministered to a Church in which the only religious way of life had been that of Christ and his gospel. When a decline set in:

It is licly that Cristis preestis, that stooden til that monkes comen, turneden to myche[1] from Cristis love, and monkes lyveden than wel beter. But thes monkes stoden awhile and turneden sonner to coveitise; and aftir monkes camen thes chanouns; and after chanouns camen freris.

All these deformed public and private worship and put their private Rules above the law of Christ, and obedience to superiors (often against the claims of charity and reason) above obedience to the Gospel. As for these founders of theirs, Augustine is undoubtedly a saint in heaven, for Wyclif has read his works, which give certain evidence of sanctity; Benedict may be there, also, though Wyclif would not be too sure of this; as for Francis and Dominic, *credat Judaeus Apella*. All have now grown rich and useless; but worst of all are the mendicants, who suck the blood of the nation and scatter heresies:

And here men noten many harmes that freris don in the Chirche. They spuyles the puple many weis by iposcrisie and other leesingis,[2] and bi this spuyling thei bilden Caymes Castelis to harme of cuntreis. Thei stelem pore mennis children, that is werse than stele an oxe; and thei stelen gladlich eires, Y leeve to speke of stelyng of wymmen... Thei moven londis to batciles,[3] and pesible persones to plete;[4] thei

---

[1] To myche: too much.　　　　　　　　[2] Leesingis: lies.

[3] This is a reference to the Flanders crusade of Bishop Spenser of Norwich in 1383; it was preached by the friars and is a frequent topic in Wyclif's tracts.

[4] Plete: plead in the courts.

maken many divorsis, and many matrimonies, unleveful,[1] bothe bi lesingis maad to parties, and bi pryvelegies of the court. Y leeve to speke of fighting that thei done in o lond and othir....And sith coventis of freris ben shrewis[2] for the more part or moche, no woundir if thei envenyme men that comes thus unto hem.

A good friar, indeed, is as rare as the phoenix.

As all such private rules of life, even when not so clearly vicious, are superfluous and harmful to the spread of the spirit of the gospel, the orders one and all must be suppressed, Caim's castles sacked, and parliament should advise the king to confiscate their possessions, which may be given back to the donors or their heirs, or used by the king for the defence of the realm. Such friars as are not wholly abandoned or heretical may find employment as parish priests or schoolmasters. Wyclif, indeed, had his programme so clearly defined in his imagination, that he more than once proposes simple tests by which the iniquity of the friars may be ascertained. The easiest way, he says, is to oblige them under penalties to put on paper, or to depose under the convent seal or before fit witnesses, exactly what their belief in the Eucharist is. Those who fail to write correctly (that is, in Wyclif's sense) or at all—and if they are faithful to the pope, they are bound so to fail—must forfeit their possessions and be avoided as heretics. A second test of the *ad hominem* kind, and simpler to apply, is to ask a Carmelite or Austin friar when his order began and then ask a Preacher or a Minor whether he agrees. This will infallibly set them by the ears, and consequently all Christians should avoid them till they all agree on the truth.

In this way, by God's help, the realm might be disembarrassed of the whole brood, and while the good work is in hand, continues Wyclif, all minor sects may be sent the same way. Hospitals would not be missed, nor chantries nor guilds;

---

[1] Unleveful: loveless. [2] Shrewis: malicious.

and, with a sense of Thorough that verges on the sublime, Wyclif throws them on the fire. What, then, of Oxford colleges? Wyclif had loved Oxford dearly—it is perhaps the only deep personal emotion he ever reveals—and in a passage, which must be the earliest of all the many tributes that have been paid to the beauty of a city that has cast her spell over so many minds, he writes of her fresh meadows and pleasant streams, her verdure 'branchy between towers', the soft airs that make of her a dwelling fit for angels, a very house of God and gate of heaven. Yet even this sweet Oxford had been deflowered by the friars; they had cast its prophet forth; he was an exile who would never see its spires again. Rue, not snapdragon, clung to the walls of Balliol, and the rector of Lutterworth swept his earliest home, along with Caim's castles, out from the new Jerusalem.

There alone did his prophetic spirit see false. To those who lived in the age that was dawning, Wyclif's diatribes and schemes may have seemed the outpouring of a mind warped by heresy or soured by disease. Caim's castles, unshaken by the distant drum, grew more splendid still. Yet medieval monasticism might well have felt a premonitory tremor throughout its frame in the years when both Wyclif and Langland were walking over its grave. With an appalling precision the fate which they foretold came upon the religious, and the programme which Wyclif had outlined was carried through to the last detail. They might scatter his ashes in the Swift, but he had not failed to be beforehand with them. He had cast his bread upon the running waters, and it returned after many days.

XX

WILLIAM MORE,
PRIOR OF WORCESTER

William More (1471–1552), the last effective prior of the cathedral monastery of Worcester, kept a day-book or Journal of his movements and expenses which allows us to watch the daily life of a monastic superior, who was also a landowner and a 'county figure', in the decades immediately before the Dissolution of the monasteries.

WILLIAM PEERS, who on entering religion took the surname of More from the hamlet near Tenbury that had been his home, was born in 1471 or 1472, and was shaven and clothed with the monastic habit in St Mary's cathedral priory in 1498. He became kitchener in 1501 and later subprior under John Wednesbury. When the latter died in 1518 he was elected prior with the approval of Richard Foxe, bishop of Winchester and at that time still a person of influence. Thenceforward for some seventeen years he kept, or rather caused to be written up for him, a day-book in which were entered in detail his receipts and expenses throughout the year. It is thus possible to follow his movements and activities week by week, to note his tastes and interests, and so to form an impression of his personality and worth.

The Journal makes it abundantly clear that during the years of his priorate William More spent comparatively little time at the cathedral priory. Though the need to supervise great estates and to live off their produce had long ago vanished with the change from an economy of exploitation to one of rents, the external pattern of the prior's life is almost identical with that of the peregrinating abbots and priors of an earlier age, with that of Abbot Wenlock of Westminster or Prior Darlington of Durham. Though More had commodious lodgings in the priory, with all facilities for hospitality, he spent the greater part of the year on his manors, no longer devising and executing an agricultural policy, but living the life of a country squire in relatively long spells of residence at three or four manor houses, which priors of the past had selected as places to be kept when other manors had been leased with hall and demesne. Thus in the accounting year 1527-8 More spent only nine weeks at the priory, which he visited for some of the greater liturgical seasons of the year, such as Christmas, Quinquagesima, Easter, the Rogations and Whitsuntide; of the forty-three weeks that remained nineteen were spent at Battenhall, a manor only a mile from the cathedral, nine at Crowle, four miles to the north-east of the city, and fifteen at Grimley, four miles to the north in the valley of the Severn. This was one of the few years in which fell no visit to London, which often took up from four to six weeks. The pattern of the year 1532-3 was much the same: eleven weeks at Worcester, fourteen at Grimley, twelve at Battenhall, ten at Crowle, two in London, and the remaining four broken with journeys to town or between one manor and another.

Prior More, in his early years in office, spent considerable sums upon setting his houses, especially those at Crowle and Grimley, in good order. He tackled Crowle, which he found 'in decay', in his very first year, and in that and the year following he spent upwards of £34 on carpentry work alone; this, in that country of half-timber houses, would account for by far the larger part of the cost of a new fabric. In the next few years most of his attention was given to Grimley, where the fabric was fairly sound, and where he was consequently able to attend to furnishings, decorations and fitting up the chapel, of which the altar was consecrated shortly after Easter

in 1523 by the bishop of Ascalon, acting for the absentee bishop
of Worcester. By this time More had returned to finish
Crowle, and in the years 1524 and 1525 the house and chapel
were glazed from top to bottom, large quantities of glass being
brought down from London and fitted by 'Edmund glasyer
of Alceter'. A further large undertaking was the hanging of
all the living rooms with painted cloth or serge. This was
bought in bulk undecorated and then painted *in situ*. Entries
such as the following are frequent: 'Item to thomas Kynge
peynter for peynting the borders in the grene chambur con-
teynyng xxxiii yeards price the yeard peynting 2d'. From
Crowle the work passed to Battenhall, which was glazed on
the grand scale in the last weeks of 1524 by 'cornesshe colsull'.
Finally, when the rooms had windows and hangings, furnishings and upholstery came pouring in, with beds, tables, bed-
spreads, cushions, sheets and table napery. When the prior had
finished, Crowle and Grimley and Battenhall, as their
inventories show, were comfortable and well appointed
houses by any standards which exclude the amenities of
modern plumbing and what are called the public utility
services.

Prior More, as can be seen, lived on a substantial and
secure income paid at regular intervals either by the tenant in
person, or through bailiffs and rent-reeves, or by one of his
own monastic officials. He carried with him a retinue of some
size: four gentlemen, ten yeomen and ten grooms, in addition
to a chaplain and monk-steward, and he maintained in addition the numerous indoor and outdoor servants that en-
cumbered every large house of the age. He had no agrarian
problems to exercise him; his unavoidable expenses consisted
primarily in finding wages and maintenance for his household,
and his only cares were for the three or four available sources
of what may be called the 'heavy' provisions—the deer park,

the fish stew, the rabbit warren and the dovecot. For each of these we have details over a long course of years. Not only are we given the numbers of deer, rabbits and pigeons delivered yearly from the manors, but we can watch the expenses of fencing, ditching, hunting and snaring. Of the fish-stews in particular a very full account is given. The ponds and moats of Crowle and Grimley and Battenhall were clearly a personal interest, almost a hobby, of the prior. What with nets and weirs and floodgates, with clearances of sedge and slime, with renewals and selections of fish, they took up a considerable amount of his time and money. Each spring, at the end of March or in early April, when Lent was nearly past, the ponds were drained and the fish counted before restocking took place, usually with fish bought elsewhere. The moat at Crowle, in particular, with a surface width of forty feet narrowing to thirty at the bottom 'from under the bruge to the formust tornell ayenst the pyggion hows' was one of the achievements of his period of office. Worcestershire is to this day a country of moated farms and manors, where the shallow pools, overhung by branches of pear or cherry, are stirred only by the moorhen or the birds of the farmyard. In the century following More's death the placid girdle of water was often to save from surprise and capture both recusant and royalist; in his more peaceful day it was regarded only as the home of tench and bream and eels. When Grimley mere was drained in 1527 there were found to have survived Lent seventeen great tench, fifty-eight store tench, seven chub, a multitude of roach, two great eels, and many small eels and pike. In the Low Week of 1532 forty-three tench, two carp, four perch and three hundred roach were put into Hallow pond; forty tench and a great number of roach and perch into the nether pond there; thirty-eight bream and twenty tench into the moat at Crowle; eighteen small pike into Ashenshall and Whitnell pools. Each expanse of water carried also its swans, and every May the prior noted their increase: 'Md. that the Eyght day of may the Eyre of Swannes withyn the mott at batnall did ley ix eggs & v of them wer Addle and iiii of the eggs wer Signetts this yere. Item the Swannes in the poole at Grymley did ley vii eggs iiij beyng addyll iij of them wer signets.'

More, indeed, when out on his manors of Crowle and Grimley, sinks deep into the landscape, and the whole cycle of village life passes before us:

> When Tom came home from labour,
> And Cisse to milking rose.

It is in 1527 that the first payment (1s. 4d.) occurs 'to the maydens at grymley for syngyng on maye day'; this became an annual expense: thus in 1528, 'on may day to maydens at grymley, 16d', and in 1531, 'rewards to them that singeth on maye mornyng men and women at grymley, 3s.' The prior in these years was at Grimley in person, but he did not escape subscriptions to vocalists elsewhere; thus in 1528 we find a shilling given 'to syngers on may day at Worcester', and eightpence 'to the maydens box at Crowle'.[1] Crowle, indeed, a village not primarily associated with music in the mind of a Worcestershire man of today, had a turn for song in early Tudor years. In 1532 a reward of 16d. goes 'to the yong men of crowle for syngyng on maii day in the morenyng', while in the same week we read: 'to the maydens of crowle for syngyng on holyrowde day [3 May] in the morenyng towards our lady light, 20d., and to other syngers 12d.' In 1533 the maidens have replaced the young men on May Day, and in 1534 the usual 16d. goes 'to vi mayds at crowle that did syng

---

[1] 'Box' here and often in the Journal is clearly a collecting-box; the term is the equivalent of our 'collection' or 'subscription'; cf. 'Christmas box'.

in the morenyng on seynt philip & Jacob day (1 May)'. At
Worcester, however, male voices predominate; thus in 1533
a shilling goes at Battenhall 'to John Acton, William parker
& John tylar for syngyng on maii morenyng' and in the same
week 16d. 'to iiii of worceter singyng men for the same
syngyng'. Another occasion celebrated with early morning
song was the dedication of the priory church, which often occurred in Whit week. Thus in 1528 there were 'iiii syngers on
our dedicacion in the morenyng', and in 1531 something of a
festival with 16d. 'to the singers of the town on our dedicacion
day in the morenyng', a shilling 'to mynstrells on our dedicacion day', and 20d. 'to dauncers of the parasshe'.

April, May and June, with their early sunshine and long
evenings, were the season for every kind of entertainment.
There were the 'iiii syngyng men craftsmen of Worceter
upon seynt georges day in the morenyng at crowle'; the
'dauncers of seynt sewthans' in Ascension week, and a whole
series of parish 'shows'. Many of the entertainments were
organized for the benefit of the church; thus the parishioners
of Grimley on one occasion prepared for Whitsuntide with
a 'churche Ale and a pley', towards which More subscribed
the large sum of 7s. 6d. Another year saw the same amount
given 'to the church Ale at kyngs Norton', while in 1530,
when More was at his native village, 4s. 6d. went to 'costs &
expenses at pensax church Ale' and 2s. 4d. 'to pleyers at the
more on the Assencion day to the uce of a churche'. Bottom
and his fellows were active about midsummer in every village;
in 1519 the last week in June saw 'rewards to Robin Whod
and hys men for getheryng to tewksbury bruge'; in 1530, in
the week after Trinity Sunday, 'the Dauncers of claynes'
received 10d. and a shilling went to 'the box of Robyn hood';
in 1531 6s. 8d. went as late as 26 July 'to the tenants of clyve,
pleying with Robyn Whot, mayde marion & other', and in

May 1535, entertainment is provided by 'Robyn Whod and little John of Ombresley'.

The climax of the village season came early in July. In 1533 More notes the gift of a noble 'in rewards to alhalland church at the pley holden at hynwycke hall seynt Thomas yeve beyng sonday and on seynt Thomas day beyng monday, which pley was kept to the profett of alhaland churche'. The characteristic event of St Thomas's Day (6 July) was not, however, a play; in 1524 a shilling goes to wine 'at the bonfire at crowle on seynt thomas yeven'. In later years more details are given; thus in 1529 the prior records that he 'spende at the boonfyre at the crosse in crowle on seynt Thomas nyght amonge the hole neypurs of the seid towne iii pens in kakes, a potell and a quarte of red wyne and a potell of sacke'. A similar celebration took place at Grimley; thus in 1529 a shilling goes 'for a potell of secke & a potell of redwyne for the bonfyre'. No details, however, are given of the refreshments provided by the much larger sums distributed 'to the wyffes of more and Newenham, of burraston and of Pensax, to make mery amongs them'.

The winter solstice, and the ten days between Christmas and the Epiphany, were another season of amusement. The pattern of the festivities included one or more dinners to the corporation of Worcester. Thus during Christmas in 1520–1 we find: 'for wyne to dyner on cristmas Day I quarte of mawmesey, 3 d. To brawne for the balyffs at nyght in the grete hall; ii dosen of wafurnes [wafers]. A potell of osey & a potell of rumney, 12 d.' The dinner was accompanied by 'carrolds' [carols] and rewards were given 'to William the Lewter for his syngyng & pleying in the cristamas wycke'. Another dinner followed a week later: 'rewarded to iiii pleyers of glowceter a pon sonday when the balyffs and the xxiiii dyned with me in the grete hall, 3 s. 4 d.' On New

Year's Day 1525 a touch of colour is given: 'At Worceter the balis & all skarlet gownes dyned with me.' In More's last year, the Christmas of 1534–5, further invitations were issued: 'the bayliffs & ther wyffs & other of the citie with ther wyffs xviii dyned with me sonday seynt Johns day.' The entry does not state what entertainment was provided, but we note: 'to mynstrells Innocents day [28 December] and a popet player 2s. 0d., to singers of carrowls, 8d., to iiii pleyers on Innocents day 2s. 8d.' On occasion the city fathers had to be satisfied with less severe amusements; 'rewards to ii childurn that tumbled before me & the balyffs & others, 12d.'

In addition to his subscriptions to the amateur theatricals of Crowle and Grimley, More found himself also patron of the professionals, strolling players and instrumentalists and conjurors of the king or queen, or of a magnate of Church or State. It might be 'the mynsrtells of my lord of Shrewsbury', the 'kyngs Jugeler and his blynd harper William More', who was to be in trouble ten years later, or maybe 'the kings pleyers John slye and his company' or 'William slye and his company beyng the queen's pleyers'. 'The kyngs Jogellar, Thomas brandon' was a frequent visitor both at Worcester and Grimley; his 'chylde' earns 8d. 'for tumblyng'; among other visitors were 'my lord cardinal's mynstrels', 'a mynstrel of sir George throckmorton', and 'the dewke of Suffolke's trumpeturs'; in lieu of a circus the prior could command 'the kyngs bereward at batnall havyng ii beres there'. When alone he had his fool, Roger Knight, whom he had seemingly inherited from his predecessor and for whom, alone of all his following, he makes individual purchases of clothes, including motley, and for whose laundry also he regularly pays. These expenses cease in 1524, when Roger may have died, and there is no indication that a successor was found. Of the prior's own recreations there is only one hint, the purchase in the summer of 1520 of 'ix bulls [bowls] to bull with all, 8 d'. We may note with interest a later entry: 'Item for a bagge pype, 2 s. 8 d.'

More, like Abbot Wenlock of Westminster and many another prelate, came from a family of middling circumstances in the countryside, and, again like Wenlock and many another son who had risen to a position of influence and wealth in the church, he maintained an affectionate and generous contact with his relatives. In his first years of office his parents came to live at Grimley and received many marks of attention; thus in 1519 we find 'to my mother 3 s. 4 d. ayenst Easter', and the same sum 'rewarded to my father & mother a yenst cristmas'. Indeed, a gift 'before I went to London', suggests that his parents were in some way dependent upon him, as does another entry 'payd to sir William chylde for 40 bus. of whete for my father's rent, 70 s'. This note is followed almost immediately by a whole series of purchases of material and payment for labour 'at my father's house at grymley'. Clearly this was a new and substantial building, with a thatched roof, but Richard Peers did not live to see the house-warming. He must in any case have been well stricken in years and he died suddenly towards the end of February 1520. When he was buried on the 20th at Grimley the little place could seldom have seen a costlier funeral: what with candles and Masses and breakfast for the monks at Worcester and sundry other provisions the obsequies brought a bill of more than £9. This, however, was exceeded when Mrs Peers died. The funeral was celebrated at Grimley manor by the black and grey friars of Worcester, in addition to a dirge at the cathedral, and Anne Peers was laid to rest in the chancel of the parish church at a cost of £10. 10 s.

The Journal has more than once taken us into the world of Mistress Ford and sweet Anne Page; as we read on we might think ourselves to be in Justice Shallow's orchard or by the table dormant in the hall of Chaucer's Franklin. Provisions must necessarily bulk large in any account book, but the impression is given by many documents of early Tudor England that they served almost as a medium of exchange or a form of accumulated wealth. Prior More records his New Year gifts for 1519: they come from a miscellaneous group of friends, clients and henchmen, ranging from the landlords of the Plough and the Cardinal's Hat to 'John yks wyff': between them they contributed twenty capons, four dozen larks, two peacocks, two peahens, two geese, eight partridges, a shoulder of brawn, one lamb, one pig, six snipe and teal, one lamprey, a dish of trout and grayling, another of roach, and two cheeses, one of them being 'grete'. This score, however, was passed easily the following year, when the total of capons was twenty-three, with five peacocks, thirteen dozen larks, six woodcock, eight partridges, one 'feysand', four 'Stikkes of birds', three geese (one of them 'green'), one duck, one cygnet, a hundred warden pears, twenty 'oregges' and two 'boxes of bisketts'. On the other hand, the presents appear to become more varied as the years pass. In 1519, the only friend who made no contribution to the larder was the abbot of Winchcombe's cousin, a mercer, who sent 'a fyne hand napkyn'. In 1532, besides game and delicacies including 'a peece of marmylade',[1] we notice 'a peyer of gloves', 'A tothe pycke garnesshed with selver & gylt', 'a pyllows bere' [=pillow case], 'a peyer of knyffes' and 'a case to putt pennes & ynke in'.

Intermingled with the material or social expenses are a fair number with a religious purpose. The friars of Worcester, black and grey, often received gifts at Christmas, sometimes of a shilling, at other times of a dish of lampreys, and there are several entries such as the following, which must represent

---

[1] The word 'marmalade' was first used of a conserve of quinces, and then for plum jam; it had a consistency like that of our 'candied' fruit.

responses to a mendicant's request: 'to the prior of the fryurs of wyche [i.e. Droitwich] when he went to his generall chapter, 8 d.' All indications, indeed, show that the friars were still poor and dependent upon charitable gifts. Besides personal gifts, a number of benefactions to churches occur. Not all these gifts went to churches belonging to Worcester priory. There are, for example, subscriptions 'to the Sextone of moche malverne to the byldyng of the parisshe churche there, 3 s. 4 d.', 'to the priur of little malverne towards the losses of his chalesses stolen, a noble'. Gifts on the occasion of a priest's first Mass are frequent, and the prior several times gave attention to the needs of an ancress, as 'payde in brycke lyme and sond to the reparacon of the Anckras hows by the charnel hows, 10s. 0d.' Cases of distress are met with help: 'rewarded to Nicholas the clerke of the church when he was Robbed, 12 d.'; 'In rewards to a por man of overbury beyng brent 12 d.'; and once a payment of 20d. is recorded 'for ii shurts to William begger a por yong man'. It may have been the spirit of the season that led the prior one Christmas week to risk a shilling in reward 'to certen persons be syde the rodes for redempcion of a gentilman in turkey'.

The yearly visit to London was used for negotiating large purchases, as well as for ordinary shopping. In 1520 the prior bought a ring, two chalices and four pieces of plate for £20, and cloth of gold and orphreys to the value of £87 for a set of vestments. In 1522 came the most costly purchase of his life, a precious mitre bought of John Cranks, goldsmith, for £49. 15s., and a pastoral staff for £28. 15s. Whether or no More heard any criticism of these large expenses at the time cannot be known, but it is worth noting that they were to be brought against him more than ten years later, and that in the remaining thirteen years of his rule he made only one purchase at all comparable to them. This was in 1525, when the acquisition of a 'grete byryles [beryl] stone with the garnesshyng of hym at london' cost £10 with a considerable further sum for carriage when, three years later, the stone came down to Worcester and was placed in position before St John's altar. It was intended to be the prior's tombstone; like many other costly monuments erected during the lifetime of eminent men it never covered the body of its purchaser.

Among the London purchases books often figured. Some were certainly bought for the convent library, others for himself. So far as can be ascertained, almost all the books purchased for cash were printed books, and many were patristic, scholastic and canonistic works that had long been classics— Seneca, Cyprian, Jerome, Gregory, Ambrose, Richard of St Victor, Aquinas, Hostiensis, Innocent IV, Zabarella. These were presumably bought as useful modern editions of books that had long been in manuscript at Worcester. A few are more personal: the prior twice bought copies of Bishop Longland's translation of the Rule of St Benedict, and copies of the English chronicles and the Life of Christ by Ludolph of Saxony may have been for private reading. On the whole, however, the number of books clearly bought to satisfy More's personal needs was small. Most notable of all in some respects is a group of five collections of early and recent statutes of England, going down to 1534. The prior, as will be seen, was for many years on the commission of peace, but the purchase may also remind us that all men in public place had to keep abreast of the prolific legislation of the Reformation Parliament.

The Journal says little of the prior's relations with his convent, and only once records the appointment of an official. We learn casually that he himself exercised the functions of kitchener in the year 1530-1, and in the latter year there was an extensive 'renewyng of disshes in the covent kychion'.

As has been noted, More spent little time at Worcester, and then only at festival seasons, when guests must have taken up most of his leisure. He appears to have given a number of customary entertainments to the community—at Christmas, at 'quytide' (Quinquagesima Sunday), and most elaborately after the Maundy on Holy Thursday, when a greater expense on wine is recorded than on any other day. He paid also regularly 10s. a quarter for the ten o'clock Mass, and 2s. 4d. yearly at Michaelmas for geese for the convent's breakfast. He had with him a chaplain and a monk-steward, to whom he paid 6s. 8d. a quarter, but of other monks we hear little. Battenhall was not. like Bearpark at Durham, a place of holiday for the brethren; the rewards 'to the iiij Novices at batnall the iii day after their profession' were probably made on the occasion of a formal visit. On the other hand, Battenhall was sufficiently near Worcester for monks to visit the prior without appearing in the accounts, and an entry occasionally occurs, when the prior is elsewhere, of sums paid to visiting brethren. The only group of these to figure at all frequently are the students at Oxford. Worcester had from the first sent a regular stream to the college—then Gloucester College—which now perpetuates the connection by its name, and it may have become customary that the prior should bear the expenses connected with the inception of masters and bachelors. Entries of such payments are not rare, as 'rewarded to dan John Lewarne to be bachelor of divinite in oxford, 40s.', and 'rewarded to dan Roger neckham to be Doctor of Divinite, 40s. 2 d.'

Two Worcester monks receive exceptional mention. The one is dan Robert Alchurche the sexton. An early entry shows him to have been trusted by More, and another, unique of its kind, notes his death 'in the Sextry a bowte vii of the clocke at nyght' on 10 December 1531. Thenceforward at intervals the prior pays a considerable sum for Masses for his soul. The other name has still more significance in the light of after events. In the autumn of 1527 and thenceforward for a considerable time, and again for a period in 1531, a series of payments is made to dan John Musard for working in the library on binding and repairing books. This is almost the only payment of its kind to a monk in the diary, and it is natural to suppose that Musard may have been in some way an object of the prior's encouragement or care—a conjecture which receives some support from the note at New Year, 1531, of a gift 'of musard a potell glasse of aquavite'. If this were so, the care was ill requited, for at midsummer, 1531, there is the entry: 'the takyng of musard. Item rewarded to Roger bury, Lewes the bedull, John tyler and Richard the cellarer's horse-keeper for the fatching and conveying dan John Musard home from overbury after he robbed his master of certen plate & other things, 6s.'

Although Prior More made no great figure in the social or political life of the country, he could not, as head of a great house and a landowner of importance, escape certain public duties. For some years he can be seen entertaining the justices at times of sessions; in 1526 he is himself of the quorum, and his first appearance on the bench is recorded by the payment of 3s. 4d. to the constable of the castle 'for the leying the quysshon [cushion] for me at the sessheons [sessions]'. Henceforward he is always at Worcester when the justices are sitting. He was also of necessity a professional dispenser of hospitality. As a rule, his guests do not appear by name in his Journal, but at Crowle and elsewhere we catch glimpses of the gentlemen of Worcestershire and Warwickshire, the Winters of Huddington and the Throckmortons of Coughton, whose descendants in the third and fourth generations were to earn a tragic notoriety. Occasionally the name of a great lady appears.

At Worcester, in the last week of August 1523, we note: 'Item for swete wyne spended upon my lady sannys, 12 s. 10 d.' Lady Sandys was a Worcestershire woman, a Bray by birth; she had married a young courtier who was to remain one of the king's favourites and to give her a beautiful home, 'The Vyne', in Berkshire. In 1530 we find her sending More a rosary: 'a peyer of grete Amber bedes of v settes', and, as we shall see, her friendship with the prior was to have issue in later years.

An exception to the casual entries of hospitality occurs in 1526. Early in that year the Countess of Salisbury, Margaret Pole, arrived with her charge, the nine-year-old Princess Mary, then still heiress presumptive of England. Her arrival was preceded by some hasty decorating, and attempts to make her apartment weather-proof, and expenses rose considerably during her stay. The princess was in the priory for five weeks, and then moved to Battenhall for a month, returning to Worcester half-way through Holy Week, and departing again after Low Sunday, her retinue being the better by £7. 13s. 4d. from gratuities received from the priory. Mary's offerings at the prior's Mass on St Wulstan's Day (19 January), Candlemas, Easter Sunday and the Assumption are recorded. The princess returned at the beginning of August and Thomas Brandon, 'the king's Joguler' was on hand; when she left the prior escorted her to Cropthorne and Evesham. Shortly before this visit there is a note of three payments for wine 'for my lady salesbury sons', one of them being 'my lord mowtigeowe'.[1] The imagination rests for a moment on the guest-hall at Worcester that year. England in 1526 must still have seemed a settled country with the future predictable, when Anne Boleyn and Thomas Cromwell were still in private place, and the sword that was to divide kinsmen so sharply lay still

[1] Mowtigeowe = Montague.

167

sheathed. Yet the four visitors who sat there with the prior were all to know sorrow, and were all in their fashion to suffer, or to cause suffering, for their faith. The Countess and her elder son were to perish at the hands of the executioner, while the younger son was to die in exile haunted by the disaster that he had helped to cause. They must often have spoken of the absent brother, Reginald, also in part to be the cause of their fate, who was himself to die, a prince of the Church, on the same day as the little girl, his cousin, each of them alone in the new, harsh world which they had hoped to sweeten, but had only the more embittered.

Other clouds were soon on the horizon. The years after 1529 were full of vital changes, with rumours of more impending, and even if we had no further knowledge, we might guess that it was not a time when a great monastery could prosper in peace of spirit while its head spent his days among the rewards and fairies of Grimley. In fact, the cathedral priory was not at peace, and the interplay within its walls of selfishness and frailty with the designs of the powerful minister, who for some years before the end had been receiving a large annual fee from the prior, might be taken as an exemplary instance of the combination of agencies that brought about the downfall of the monasteries. Sources of friction and weakness, which had existed for decades or centuries without fatal consequences, were now to bring the fabric down.

Explosive material had long been lying about in the priory of St Mary, but fifty years before it would probably never have been touched off. As so often happened, the train was fired by the royal visitation of 1535. This took place on 1 August, and was conducted by Dr Legh and Ap Rice, for both of whom it was a new experience. Before them the various parties in the priory aired their grievances freely, above all Musard, an unworthy protégé of the prior, and Fordham the deposed cellarer, who besides their personal wrongs took the opportunity of denouncing one of their brethren, Dan Richard Clyve, for criticizing the statute of appeals, railing against the king and Queen Anne, alluding to the king as a weather-cock and upholding Queen Katharine and the authority of the pope. The visitors in their inexperience took a very reasonable view of all this, and agreed with the prior's poor opinion of Musard; he found himself in prison once more and his attempts to write to Cromwell were successfully frustrated for a time. Finally, he succeeded in getting letters off to both the king and Cromwell, denouncing his confrère, Dan Richard, and his prior. 'As a religious man', he remarked, 'I felt bound to send the words of treason and the cloaking of them by my master', and he swept up a long list of charges against More, 'my unkind master', including one of unlawfully deposing Fordham and Neckham 'for standing unto the right of the house'. Fordham for his part joined in the denunciation and offered Cromwell one hundred marks if he might be restored to office. A charge of treason against a superior was always acceptable to the government, as it simplified negotiations for surrender, and Cromwell lost no time in submitting the alleged treasonable words to Audley in London. The chancellor, however, gave a lawyer's cautious reply: the reference made by Clyve to the weathercock could hardly bear an interpretation of treason; misprision of treason was the most that could be hoped for. As for the criticism of the king and Queen Anne at Christmas time, the words had unfortunately been spoken a month too soon, as the date fixed for the operation of the penalties under the Treasons Act had been 1 February. The best course would be to have an indictment made out and then to take evidence and wait. Audley followed this up by sending the necessary instrument down to Worcester.

The case was duly heard by Rowland Lee and the dossier sent up to London. Prior More meanwhile was sent to Gloucester Abbey under house arrest, but Lee wrote to Cromwell that caution was needed in going to extremes with such a well-known figure in county society as the prior of Worcester; he was 'a great possessioner, and at assizes the gentry of the county had been familiarly entertained by him'. Meanwhile, wires were being pulled in every direction. The community of Worcester were in no mind to have Fordham back again as cellarer and sent a round robin with twenty-eight signatures to Cromwell telling him so. On the other hand, Cranmer down at Canterbury only a fortnight after the visitation had got wind of what had happened. He understands, so he writes to Cromwell, that the priory of Worcester is shortly to be void; if so, he hopes the vicar-general will be good to Dr Holbeach, a monk of Crowland and prior of the student monks at Cambridge, where the archbishop had known him. As for More, he found a good friend in his guest of other years, Lady Margery Sandys, whom we have seen in the past taking a glass of wine with the prior and sending him a valuable rosary. She wrote to Cromwell warmly on his behalf, demanding that the matter should be looked into at once, and judiciously adding to her forthright advocacy the assurance that the prior, 'a true monk to God and his King', would doubtless 'be glad to give you in ready money as much as any other man will give'. She could speak with the greater boldness, for less than a week before writing she had acted as hostess to the king and Queen Anne at the Vyne. She had probably brought More's name up during the royal visit, for the king was disposed, we hear, 'through pity' to restore More to office; before doing so, he told Cromwell to find out the views of the new bishop of Worcester, Hugh Latimer. Latimer for some reason was not More's friend, and with rather less than his traditional bluntness of speech he let it be understood that he did not want the old prior back. More did in fact return early in 1536, but he seems to have shown some resentment towards those of his brethren who had caused all the trouble. In any case, Musard was active once again with a sheet of charges which readers of the prior's Journal will recognize as resting on a basis of fact, even if they are extremely stale and essentially unfair. The prior, Musard tells Cromwell, maintains his relatives and retinue of twenty-four attendants in comfort while the monks want. 'I wish you knew', he adds feelingly, 'of the poor service the convent has on fish days.' The prior takes land from his tenants to enlarge his parks, and wastes money on hospitality and litigation in London while 'your cloister' crumbles. Above all, he has bought quite unnecessarily a precious mitre and staff, and Musard who, as we have seen, took an interest in plate, adds that More had been forced to sell some to pay off the debt.

The documents do not tell us what happened next. It may be that Cromwell felt that More, though clearly innocent of crime, had too many enemies and rivals for a quiet life. Possibly the prior himself realized that now or never was the time for a deal. He did in fact resign within a few weeks on favourable terms, and at the end of March 1536, Dr Holbeach succeeded him as Cranmer had wished. Nevertheless, something had biased Cromwell in More's favour; it may be that Lady Margery remained in the background at the king's ear; certainly the word went round influential circles that More's debts would be paid, and the ex-prior himself is found laying down very precisely to Cromwell what he wants: the mansion at Grimley with a suitable amount of land; a pension to be paid quarterly, and all his gear and plate and chapel stuff to go with him. An agreement was duly drawn up and signed by More, the convent and the representative of the king which embodies all these requests save one: Crowle, not Grimley, was allotted as his dower.

There behind his moat, among the nymphs and shepherds of Crowle, 'between the vale of Evesham and the woodland, deepe in the one, and warme by the other', the old man passed what years remained to him in that pleasant land of orchards, in his half-timbered manor house with its chapel and glass and its comfortable rooms, with the magnificent profile of the Malvern Hills framing his horizon when he looked towards his old home at Worcester. Many years before he had ordered his tomb before the altar of the Jesus chapel in the cathedral of St Mary, but when his hour came it was in Alveston church, and under a simpler stone, that he was laid.

XXI

JOHN HOUGHTON AND
THE LONDON CARTHUSIANS

John Houghton (? 1488–1535), was the last authentic prior of the London Charterhouse. A man of great holiness of life and exceptional gifts as a leader, he refused, along with seventeen of his community, to take the Oath of (Royal) Supremacy, renouncing the pope, in 1535, and was executed at Tyburn.

ALTHOUGH the history of the London Charterhouse in the fifteenth century may not have been remarkable, the situation of the place, so different from that of the earliest and latest foundations of the province, must always have ensured a certain celebrity for its withdrawn and austere vocation. It would seem in consequence to have attracted throughout the period a steady flow of recruits with a genuine desire for a life of monastic perfection; it also attracted—as the Carthusian order has always attracted from the days of St Hugh to our own—a number of aspirants of enthusiastic or neurotic temperaments some of whom succeeded, then as now, in winning through at least the early stages of the difficult probation, to prove a source of infinite vexation to all in authority by their mental and moral vagaries, and by their graceless, spiteful or ill-grounded accusations against those who had endeavoured to wean them, and to protect others, from their habits of selfishness and irresponsibility.

Among the genuine vocations of the later fifteenth century was one which perhaps did more than any other to determine the subsequent fortunes of the house; it was that of William Tynbygh or Tenbi, Irish or Anglo-Irish by race, and of good family, who joined the community *c.* 1470 and became prior in 1500, holding office for thirty years. Tynbygh had experienced a radical conversion as a young man, and his subsequent life was ascetic to a degree; it was no doubt he who set up in the house such a high standard of fidelity to the statutes of the order. It was shortly before Tynbygh's rule began that the young Thomas More lived in the precincts for four years; it was Tynbygh who received John Houghton into the community, and it was in his last years that there set in a remarkable flow of ardent and distinguished recruits who were to form the core of the resistance to the king in 1534.

Lying as it did at the edge of the city, with its orchards and gardens running up among the town houses of the great, the Charterhouse could scarcely fail to be a centre of religious influence. The solemn devotion of the liturgy, the contrast between the silence and austerity there and the noisy, restless, ambitious and sordid whirl of the city streets, the presence within its walls of a number of men of gentle birth and high abilities, attracted to its gatehouse many of the *âmes d'élite* of the time, and facilities seem to have been given for those in need of spiritual direction to visit and confess themselves to the priests, and even to make a prolonged stay in the guest quarters.

Tynbygh was succeeded by Dom John Batmanson, who was a man of sufficient learning to be chosen by Edward Lee, the friend of More and future archbishop of York, to criticize the edition of the New Testament by Erasmus. That hypersensitive scholar's reaction to Batmanson's attack need not be taken as a pondered judgment, but the Carthusian, who continued his work with an attack on Luther and who wrote treatises in the medieval manner on passages of Scripture, was clearly not one of the new learning and was probably no match for its masters. In any case, his rule was short.

In his successor, John Houghton, the strict monastic life brought to blossom for the last time on English soil a character of the rarest strength and beauty—a last flowering, a winter rose, of English medieval monachism. When all allowance is made for the youthful hero-worship and later hagiological aim of Maurice Chauncy, the picture that emerges is of a man capable not only of inspiring devoted attachment, but of forming in others a calm judgment and a heroic constancy equal to his own. He found himself head of a family in which youth was predominant; more than half the community were under the age of thirty-five when he began his short rule; no doubt they were impressionable enough. But it was not the most impressionable who followed him to the end of his journey; Chauncy and others like him were left orphans, remembering with sorrow the golden days of spring; the seventeen who did not fail had learnt from him to depend on no human guide, to fear neither sharp pain nor material want, and to be true, through all extremes of suffering and desola-tion, to the purpose of their profession.

Houghton had joined the Charterhouse early in the reign of Henry VIII. Sprung of gentle family in Essex, he had taken a degree in laws at Cambridge from Christ's College, but instead of embarking on a career, he had studied in retirement for the priesthood and lived for some years as a secular priest before taking the monastic habit in 1515. Seven years later he became sacrist and after five more years, to his great distress, he was appointed to the distracting office of procurator. From this he was taken, in 1530–1, to be prior of Beauvale in Nottinghamshire, but after a bare six months he was recalled by the unanimous vote of the community, in 1531, to become prior of the London house.

As prior he was able to develop his character to the full. Much of Chauncy's long account of his virtues is wordy and conventional, but a few individual traits can be clearly seen. The prior, we are told, was reserved and somewhat stern with aspirants for the first few years of their training; with the elder fathers, jealous, as always in a strict community, of custom and precedent, he was tactful and easy of approach. Mindful of his position in public, he required an exact performance of the ceremonial of courtesy and respect; when he entered another's cell he put his dignity aside and spoke as an equal, not as a superior. His life was abstemious beyond the demands of the Rule, and he had an exceptionally deep love of the Office, in which he noticed the least haste or failure, and would even leave the choir as a sign of disapproval. An extant letter of his is witness that he followed the contemporary stream of his order's devotion, and esteemed highly Denis the Carthusian; his confessor, however, was William Exmew, who is known to have prized highly *The Cloud of Unknowing* and its companion treatises, and the younger man may have taken his bent from his superior. Houghton was regarded as a saint by those who knew him in the years when a martyr's death for one in the London Charterhouse would have seemed an impossibility. Whatever his methods, he achieved a result rare in any religious order and most rare, perhaps, in one long established and rooted in tradition: he joined his community to himself in a new and joyful realization of the splendour of their vocation and in an ever-fresh, never-failing hope of a still nearer approach to God. Before the sudden gathering of the clouds, when the world outside seemed full of costly splendour and empty show, and of the 'packs and sets of great ones', the House of the Salutation was a green valley where those of goodwill could find pasture and clear water. In Chauncy's pages, written when the old age had gone downstream in the cataclysm, there is a poignant, if inarticulate, cry to Time to cease his passage: *Verweile doch, du bist so schön.*

The monks whom Houghton guided were as a body worthy of their prior. He himself looked upon them as angels of God, and visitors who sought of them counsel and help involuntarily echoed the words of the patriarch: 'Verily God is in this place.' It was commonly said that if a man wished to hear the divine service carried out with due reverence he should visit the London Charterhouse. The rules of fasting and silence were kept in their strictness, and such alleviation as the fire in the cell were often forgone save in extreme cold. The night choirs in winter, when the lessons were long, began shortly after ten and lasted till three in the morning. Fear of distraction was so real among the brethren that the intention had been formed of asking the king to take over ownership of the property of the house, allowing the monks only a pension from it.

The life of the Charterhouse, contrasting as it did so strongly with the turmoil of the city and the display of the court and of the cardinal of York, and with the worldliness of so much in the church life of the country, could not but prove a powerful magnet to what generous aspirations still existed. Chauncy tells us that many of the monks were of wealthy or distinguished family, and that many even of the lay brethren had given up property or the expectation of affluence in order to enter the house. Though his canons of distinction may have been those of a bourgeois rather than of an aristocrat, his statement can in several cases, besides that of Chauncy himself, be corroborated from his own pages or other sources.

After Houghton, the figure most clearly seen is that of William Exmew. Like his prior, he was of good family and a Cambridge man of exceptional ability; at the Lady Margaret's recent foundation of Christ's College he had become familiar with Greek as well as Latin. In 1534 he was still but twenty-eight, though distinguished by both ability and holiness; he had been first vicar (or second in command) and then procurator of the house, while Houghton's choice of him as confessor is a sufficient proof of his maturity and spiritual insight. The impressionable Chauncy, to whom Exmew in his radiant young manhood appeared the *beau idéal* of a monk, has recorded several personal details of him, and in particular of his self-reproach as he, the procurator, left the night-choirs early, likening himself to Judas who was unworthy to hear the last words of his Master. More valuable still, perhaps, is the evidence of a manuscript that Exmew knew well, and nourished his spirit on, *The Cloud of Unknowing*, which he caused Chauncy to copy.

Yet a third, like Exmew still young, has left a mark on the records of the time. Sebastian Newdigate, bearer of a name which since his day has more than once left a notable impress on English life, sprang of a family settled at Harefield in Middlesex and later also at Arbury in Warwickshire. Through his mother, Dame Amphylis Nevill, he was related to the county families of Lincolnshire; an elder sister Jane, who married Sir Robert Dormer, was ancestress of a family ever to be distinguished among the English Catholics; another sister, mother of the recusant Lady Stonor, stood at the head of a long line faithful to the old allegiance; two brothers were knights of Malta and two other sisters became nuns in the observant convents of Syon and Dartford. The young Sebastian, tall, handsome, gallant and with great charm of manner, had gone to court as a page, where he attracted the notice of the king and became a gentleman of the Privy Chamber. When the royal divorce was first mooted his sister, Lady Dormer, summoned him to visit her and warned him of the danger of the king's example. The young courtier at first defended his master, but finally promised that if his sister's judgment proved correct, he would remember her advice. 'Remember it and act upon it', she retorted. 'I shall', he said. 'I fear for you', she replied. He paused, leaning his head upon his hand, and then asked what she would think if she heard that he had become a Carthusian monk. 'A monk,' rejoined his affectionate sister, 'I fear, rather, I shall see thee hanged.' A few months later, Newdigate was in the Charterhouse, though Lady Dormer would not be persuaded of the authenticity of his conversion till she had called upon Tynbygh herself.

Chauncy tells us, and those with any experience of observant religious communities will readily believe his words, that the converses fell not a whit short of the choir monks in holiness. He says—and this again is a familiar experience—that many were men of prayer and often surprised the more learned by the spiritual wisdom with which they spoke of what they had heard read in church or refectory. In the event, a number of them proved able to hold their own even more successfully than the choir monks in confessing their faith and in the endurance of prolonged suffering.

The Carthusians, in common with all other subjects of the king, were required in the spring of 1534 to swear to the first Act of Succession, and by so doing to acquiesce in the annulling of Henry's first marriage and in the legitimization of Anne Boleyn's offspring. Their sympathies had unquestionably lain with Queen Katharine, and they were personally persuaded of the validity of her marriage; when the commissioners first arrived on 4 May to tender the oath Houghton replied in the name of all that what the king might do was no business of Carthusians; they asked only to be left in their peace. When urged to assemble the community to swear he replied that he could not see how such a long-standing marriage could be declared invalid. He was therefore conveyed to the Tower along with the procurator Humphrey

Middlemore. There they were visited by Edward Lee, archbishop of York, and others, and persuaded that the faith was not at stake; it is possible that they never saw the preamble to the Act, with its implicit repudiation of papal authority, which formed the obstacle in the way of More and Fisher; in any case they agreed to take the oath, so far as it might be lawful, and were sent home. They had, however, gone too fast for the community, most of whom were still for refusing to swear. When the commissioners returned to administer the oath, they apparently obtained no adhesions; at a second visit, Houghton and half a dozen swore, and it was only at a third visit, at the prior's instant wish and surrounded by men-at-arms, that all took the oath. So far as can be seen, their opposition rested on a strong disapproval of the king's action rather than on a clear sight of the ultimate principles involved; when they swore, therefore, it was without doing utter violence to their consciences in a matter of faith.

Houghton's expressed forebodings that they would not long be left in peace were speedily realized. In the same session of Parliament the Treason Act was passed, which extended the definition of that crime to include treason by word, and specifically such speech as might 'maliciously' deprive the king of any of his 'dignities or titles'. Under this act, which came into force on 1 February 1535, a charge of high treason could be brought against anyone who denied, or who even refused to acknowledge, that the king was Supreme Head on earth of the Church in England. No oath was attached to the act, but in the spring of 1535 commissioners were appointed to require acknowledgment of the king's headship of the Church, and this was usually obtained by administering an oath upon the gospels in general terms of acceptance of the king's headship. All religious houses were visited for this purpose in due course.

PLATE VII

JOHN HOUGHTON

PLATE VIII

EVESHAM ABBEY

When it was clear that they would not be ignored the Carthusians realized that the day of trial had come. Houghton's chief anxiety was for the many young members of his community whose vocations he had doubtless fostered and whose professions he had received. He feared for their perseverance if the house were suppressed, and he even considered the possibility of outward compliance, with words of reservation, in order to save his monastery if he alone could swear for all. Meanwhile, he set aside three days of preparation for the trial: on the first, all made a general confession; on the second all, led by Houghton himself, asked pardon of each of his brethren in turn for all offences; on the third, the prior sang a Mass of the Holy Spirit for guidance. When he did so, and the moment came for the elevation of the consecrated Host, all felt in their hearts, and to some it seemed that they heard, either as a gust of wind or as an echo of harmony, a breath of the Spirit Whose counsel they had implored. The celebrant was for some minutes unable to continue the Mass, and at the subsequent chapter he spoke of his experience thankfully indeed, but with an exhortation that all should abide in God's grace with prayer, humble and fearful. His own constant prayer was that of Christ for his disciples: 'Holy Father, keep them whom thou hast given me in thy name.'

While Houghton thus awaited the summons he was visited by his fellow priors of Beauvale and Axholme. The former, Robert Laurence, was in origin a monk of London; the latter, Augustine Webster, had professed at Sheen. They decided to forestall the commissioners by seeking an interview with Cromwell in which to ask for exemption from the obligation of the oath. This was refused, and after a series of three interrogations conducted by the vicar-general they were lodged for their pains in the Tower, where Fisher and More already ay on the matter of the Oath of Succession, and were examined by some of the Council. Houghton took careful notes of their various examinations, and these, after being read by Fisher, were conveyed to the Charterhouse, where Chauncy saw them. Unfortunately, these papers have not survived, but Chauncy's account may be presumed to be essentially trustworthy. According to him, when they expressed willingness to consent 'so far as the law of God might allow', Cromwell roughly brushed aside all qualifications; when they asserted that the Church had always held otherwise, and that St Augustine had set the authority of the Church above that of Scripture, the vicar-general replied that he cared naught for the Church and that Augustine might hold as he pleased. All he wished to know was whether they would swear a direct oath or no. They then refused absolutely. It seems clear that in taking this decision they were influenced solely by their conviction that a matter of divine faith was at stake. The Carthusian Order, as such, was in no direct dependence upon the papacy, as were the orders of friars, nor did the pope figure in their statutes. Nor had Houghton and his companions any concern with the unity of Christian nations, whatever may have been the case with More. All that Chauncy says, and all that can be extracted from the fragments of Houghton's notes and record sources, goes to show that the Carthusian priors and their followers, many of them men of education and wide reading, stood purely and simply by the traditional faith of the Church in the divine commission to Peter. They were thus in the most literal sense martyrs of the faith.

They were in due course tried in Westminster Hall on 28–29 April, and an unwilling jury was browbeaten by Cromwell into pronouncing the verdict of guilty. After their condemnation Cranmer made one of his characteristically cautious attempts to save their lives at the expense of their convictions, but his offer to argue with them was not acceptable to Cromwell. As they left the Tower for Tyburn on a May morning (Tuesday, 4 May) they did not know that they were watched by one who had long known them and wished them well. With his customary humility More, who was standing with his daughter by a window, attributed their early release from this world's prison to the long years of penance they had spent while he had lived at ease, and he called the attention of his Margaret to their joyful alacrity, as of men going to their marriage. By the royal command they were executed in their monastic habits, with the hair shirts of their Rule beneath. Each at the foot of the gallows was offered pardon if he would submit, and on their refusal the barbarous sentence was carried out with every circumstance of cruelty. Houghton, the first to die, embraced his executioner and addressed the vast crowd, taking them to witness against the day of judgment that he died rather than deny the teaching of God's Church. He bore the agony of the butchery, aggravated by the tough hair shirt, with what seemed a more than human patience; conscious to the end, he died invoking the Lord he had loved and followed to the Cross. He was forty-eight years of age.

When the prior had been taken to the Tower the government of the House of the Salutation fell to the vicar, Humphrey Middlemore, who acted in all things with the counsel of the procurator, William Exmew, and of Sebastian Newdigate. On the very day of the execution Cromwell sent his 'owne Thomas Bedyll' to the Charterhouse, furnished with copious anti-papal literature. The three seniors, at his request, spent the rest of the day perusing the books, but found nothing in them to alter their convictions. Bedyll, meanwhile, had been taken sick, but he summoned the Carthusians to his bedside and warned them of the dangers of hypocrisy and vainglory, not to speak of the direct action of the lying spirit who had deceived the prophets of Achab. Still unconvinced, the three monks were removed to the Marshalsea, where they remained for a fortnight chained by the neck and legs to posts without the possibility of moving or the relief of a minute's freedom. Here, according to a tradition which may be reliable, Newdigate, the ex-courtier, received a visit from his old master, who made a last attempt to win his submission by alternate blandishments and threats. But neither fair words nor the frown of the instant tyrant could shake the Carthusian, and in due course this second trio were examined by the Council and (11 June) tried at Westminster. Gallant, high-spirited young men as they were, unbroken by their long ordeal of pain, they adhered steadfastly to their refusal and put forth their reasons with energy and ability. A week later (19 June), like the three priors, they went to their death as to a feast, with eagerness and joy.

The oppression of the monks remaining in the Charter-house lasted for two years. There is evidence that the king would have made short work of the opposition earlier, but that Cromwell, presumably for reasons of policy, was un-willing to outrage public sentiment with the spectacle of the sudden and complete destruction of a community so highly esteemed, and therefore delayed long to accomplish the royal wishes. At last, however, the king became more instant, and in May 1537, a division was at last effected in the sorely tried family. The Council threatened to suppress the house out of hand, and a number of the monks, exhausted by the persecu-tion and hoping to save their monastery, agreed to renounce the authority of the pope and to accept that of the king as supreme head; this they swore to so far as words went though, if we may believe Chauncy who was ultimately one of their number, their hearts and consciences always gave the lie to their lips. It was not, however, thus with all. Ten remained, 'unmoved, unshaken, unseduced, unterrified', who would not swear; three were priests, one a deacon, and six were converses. They were immediately lodged in a filthy ward of Newgate; it was the Friday before Whitsunday, 18 May.

The first martyrs had been executed as a public spectacle. The publicity had not told against them, and the second group had been dispatched without advertisement. The third and most numerous band was denied even the dignity of a formal trial and execution. They had asked to live as hidden servants of Christ; they died, silent witnesses to his words, hidden from the eyes of all. Chained without possibility of movement in a foul atmosphere, and systematically starved, they were thus left, as Bedyll put it, to 'be dispeched by thand of God'. Abandoned by all, and dying slowly of hunger and fever, they received a moiety of succour and a more precious instance of love from a devoted woman. Margaret Gigs, the adopted daughter of Sir Thomas More, had learnt from him to practise charity and knew well of her father's admiration for the Carthusians. She now bribed her way to their prison and, acting the part of a milkmaid, carried in a bucket on her head food, which she placed with her own hands between their lips. Besides food, she brought also clean linen which she put on them, and cleansed them as they stood unable to move hand or foot. The effects of her ministration betrayed her; the authorities, finding the prisoners still alive, reprimanded the gaoler and Mistress Clement (as she now was) was denied entrance. Undeterred, she obtained access to the roof and endeavoured, by removing some tiles, to let food down in a basket. She failed in her design, and the Carthusians died one by one through the summer months; the last to die in chains was Thomas Johnson on 20 September, but a converse,

William Horne, was for some reason removed to a more tolerable durance and lived on in prison till he was drawn to Tyburn to suffer as his prior had done on 4 August 1540. 'And so this child, tried longer and more severely than any other, followed his father, and died for the love of Jesus, and for the faith of his bride the Catholic Church', thus completing the tale of eighteen martyrs, for two of those exiled from London had been hanged at York in 1537.

Rarely indeed in the annals of the Church have any confessors of the faith endured trials longer, more varied or more bitter than these unknown monks. They had left the world, as they hoped, for good; but the children of the world, to gain their private ends, had violated their solitude to demand of them an approval and a submission which they could not give. They had long made of their austere and exacting Rule a means to the loving and joyful service of God; pain and desolation, therefore, when they came, held no terrors for them. When bishops and theologians paltered or denied they were not ashamed to confess the Son of Man. They died faithful witnesses to the Catholic teaching that Christ had built his Church upon a rock.

XXII

ROBERT HOBBES,
ABBOT OF WOBURN

Robert Hobbes (d. 1538), the last abbot of the Cistercian abbey of Woburn, was executed for using words implying papal supremacy and impugning the validity of the marriage of Henry VIII and Katharine of Aragon.

WOBURN ABBEY, as we see the glimpses of its daily life in the depositions of its monks, was a respectable house of fair observance. The abbot, Robert Hobbes, was a man of some learning and knowledge of theology, with a clear mind and a kindly, reasonable disposition. He was on friendly terms with Lord Grey of Wilton and his wife, as well as with his own high steward, the gifted, susceptible, dissolute, 'eternally young' court poet and intimate friend of Henry VIII, Sir Francis Bryan. He had a conservative, wholly Catholic out-look and saw, with both clarity and sorrow, the disappearance of the religious life and of the old orthodoxy. He had taken the oath to accept the king as Supreme Head in 1534, but it had been against his conscience and, unlike others, he had never thereafter enjoyed complete peace of mind. Before giving up his papal bulls he had caused copies to be taken, and when commanded to erase the pope's name from service books he had preferred to strike it out, believing that sooner or later the tide would turn; he read and passed on to his friends a tract *De potestate Petri* composed by a priest in the neighbourhood. When the Carthusians were executed he had pronounced solemnly to his monks in chapter: 'Brethren this is a perilous time; such a scourge was never heard since Christ's passion', and he had ordered them to recite the psalm *Deus venerunt gentes* prostrate daily before the high altar. A year later, when the lesser houses were suppressed, he had enjoined the singing of the anthem *Salvator mundi salva nos*, with special prayers at Mass. When preaching he stated that the pope's jurisdiction had been abrogated 'by common consent of the realm', but never alleged Scripture to prove the king's title or the justice of the act that had taken away the power of the bishop of Rome. At Passiontide, 1538, he was seriously ill and in great pain with strangury, and when he heard that hard things were being said against those who still held for the pope he exhorted the monks round his bed to keep charity, quoting a passage from St Bernard's letter to Eugenius III: 'Other churches have each their own shepherd; thou art shepherd of the shepherds themselves', and he exhorted them never to surrender their monastery or change their religious habit. When in great physical pain from his illness, he was heard to reproach himself for failing to die with the good men who had died for holding with the pope, and he repeated that his conscience grudged him daily for his failure; whereupon one of his monks rejoined (or said that he had rejoined): 'If he be disposed to die for that matter, he may die as soon as he will.'

It is indeed clear that Abbot Hobbes was consistently opposed to all religious innovation, and that he had criticized the Boleyn marriage, the suppression of the lesser monasteries, and the tacit encouragement of heretical books. His community was divided. Some were favourable to the New Learning, and successfully objected to any public manifestation of sympathy with the cause of the Carthusians. Others had been equally, though more intemperately, outspoken in their criticism of the government; among these the subprior and Dan Lawrence Blunham were notable, and the latter had paraded his achievement in evading the formal act of swearing to the king as Supreme Head; there had been a press of monks touching the book of the gospels and he had not put out his hand. Altogether, six monks besides the abbot were noted as 'papists'.

With a community thus divided against itself the chances were great that sooner or later the recalcitrants would be delated to Cromwell. The fateful step was in fact taken by an ex-friar, William Sherburne, who for almost a year had been curate of the parish chapel at Woburn. He was, like so many of his brethren, of the New Learning, and had had several brushes with the abbot, who took him to task for his violent language:

Sir William, I heard say ye be a great railer. I marvel that ye rail so. I pray you teach my cure the scripture of God, and that may be to their edification. I pray you leave such railing. Ye call the Pope a bere and a bawson.[1] Either he is a good man or an ill. *Domino suo stat aut cadit*.[2] The office of a bishop is honourable. What edifying is this to rail? Let him alone.

The chaplain bore malice, and discovered some papal bulls in his chapel that had not been surrendered. With them, and a letter setting forth the abbot's pro-papal utterances, con-tributed by the discontented Dan Robert Salford, he went up to London to call upon the Lord Privy Seal. On his return, he informed the abbot of his errand, and was forthwith dis-missed from his cure. It was too late. Cromwell sent down Dr Petre and John Williams to take depositions and the abbot and two monks, the subprior and Dan Lawrence, were duly tried at Abbot's Woburn a month later (14 June). There was no difficulty in securing a conviction; the legal case was clear. The two monks retracted all they had said, pleaded a change

---

[1] Bere = bear; bawson = badger. The two words are found in con-junction in another example in *O.E.D.*, *s.v.* bauson.

[2] 'To his own master he standeth or falleth.' Cf. Rom. xiv. 4.

of heart and asked for mercy, all to no purpose. It has been alleged that Abbot Hobbes likewise gave way. He was certainly an ailing, broken man, and it is extremely difficult to extract a precise meaning from the long and sometimes rambling depositions, or to separate what he was alleged to have said or done from what he actually admitted, and to distinguish between retractions on matters of principle and apologies for bluntness of speech and misunderstandings. He certainly retracted an opinion he had expressed as to the 'unlawfulness' of Cranmer's acts of jurisdiction. On the other hand, he committed himself, apparently without recantation, to some very strong statements about the suppression of monasteries, the distribution by Cromwell of heretical books, and the royal divorce. His indictment at least is clear. He had stated, as recently as the previous 10 January, that 'The Bysshop of Rome's Auctorite is good and lawful within this Realme accordyng to the old trade, and that is the true waye. And the contrary of the kynges parte but usurpacion disceyved by flattery and adulacion.' He had likewise on the same occasion said: 'Yt is a mervelous thyng that the Kynges grace could not be contented with that noble quene his very true and undowted wyffe quene Kateryn.' At his trial he attempted no defence and admitted his technical guilt on both counts. No appeal for mercy or recantation of his has been preserved, nor is there record of his asking pardon for these specific statements. In the past he had certainly failed to hold to his convictions; he may have failed again, but there is no proof that he did so. Writers in the past, unaware of the precise terms of his indictment, have dwelt, perhaps unduly, on his weakness of character. They have failed to do justice to a certain elevation of mind, and absence of levity, that distinguishes him from most of the gossips and grumblers of the cloister. More than this cannot be said. *Domino suo stat aut cadit.* He was duly executed, and his abbey confiscated by attainder. The architects and landscape gardeners in their work on and about the majestic ducal mansion that perpetuated the name of Woburn Abbey were successful in obliterating every trace of the medieval past, but the oak from which the last abbot, according to a venerable tradition, was hanged continued until the early decades of the nineteenth century to stand within a stone's throw of the house.

XXIII

JOHN FECKENHAM,
LAST ABBOT OF WESTMINSTER

John Feckenham (c. 1515–85) was originally a monk of Evesham and as such studied with distinction at Oxford. At the Dissolution he obtained a benefice and later became chaplain to Bishop Bonner of London. Always a conservative in his opinions, he was in high favour in Queen Mary's reign; appointed Dean of St Paul's, he resigned the post in order to return to monastic life as abbot of the reformed Westminster Abbey. When the Abbey was again suppressed by Elizabeth I he refused to take the new oath of Royal Supremacy and was under restraint for most of the remainder of his life.

JOHN HOMAN, or, as he was known from his noviciate onwards, John Feckenham, was a native of the small village of that name on the eastern border of Worcestershire in the heart of the Midlands. From the Ridgeway, a mile or so distant, which marks the western limit of Warwickshire, the eye can travel over the forest of Arden eastwards to the uplands of Northamptonshire and Oxfordshire, and westwards across the wooded Severn valley to Brown Clee in Shropshire and the Malverns throwing their shadow over Herefordshire. Though he left his home in boyhood, and knew many vicissitudes of fortune, this man of Worcestershire was to return to Feckenham in manhood and to remember it in the last days of his extreme old age.

John Homan was born c. 1512–15 and came of well-to-do yeoman stock. His father and uncle, both with large families, died possessed of considerable property scattered about the district and often held in partnership; they were clearly the second or third generation of a peasant ancestor who had bettered himself. The boy John, possibly patronized by the Throckmortons of Coughton, four miles away in the Arrow valley, entered Evesham Abbey and proceeded as a young monk to Gloucester College at Oxford. There in the years between 1533 and 1538 he became the admired leader of a group of young student monks, one of whom was the writer of a letter-book that has survived. He proceeded B.D. in 1539, having passed through most of his theological course immediately after Cromwell's commissioners had purged Oxford of Duns Scotus and his fellows. Feckenham, on the fringe of Erasmian humanism but never one for the New Learning of Germany, had accepted the royal supremacy with the rest and had presumably acquiesced in the surrender of Evesham. He had indeed shown himself a child of this world wise in his generation, for on the very day of the surrender of the abbey a proxy was admitted on his behalf to the vicarage of Feckenham. He held the benefice for at least fourteen years, though the evidence for his residence in his cure is scanty and indirect, and he made good use of his time to become chaplain, first to John Bell, bishop of Worcester, of whose cathedral the last abbot of Evesham was dean, and then to Edward Bonner, another Worcestershire man, now bishop of London. It was as Bonner's chaplain that he entered the lists of controversy in the capital where, on 16 January 1547, a few days before the death of Henry VIII, he preached an anti-Protestant sermon at Paul's Cross deploring heresy and German novelties. For this, and also probably for refusing to accept the new doctrine of justification by faith and the abolition of fasting in Lent, as well as by reason of his close connection with Bonner, he was sent to the Tower. His release took place very early in Mary's reign, for he preached at Paul's Cross at the coronation on 23 September 1553. His fame and his reputation for orthodoxy must have grown during his imprisonment, for from the very beginning of Mary's reign he was the official preacher in London; on 6 October he was one of those chosen by Convocation to defend the doctrine of the Real Presence and Transubstantiation, and for the next six years sermon followed sermon at close intervals. Early in 1554 he visited the imprisoned Princess Elizabeth and advocated clemency to the queen, and a little later was sent to exercise his gifts of persuasion upon Lady Jane Grey. The prisoner acknowledged his eloquence but remained unmoved, and the two parted with mutual assurances that they would never meet beyond the grave, but it is pleasant to hear that when on the day of execution Feckenham attended her on the scaffold, the seventeen-year-old victim of the follies and ambitions of her elders took his hand and thanked him: 'God will requite you, good sir, for your humanity to me, though it gave me more uneasiness than all the terrors of my approaching death', and that she turned to him to ask whether she might say the *Miserere* before she died.

Thenceforward for the rest of the reign he was constantly in demand for sermons and disputations, and as a member of royal commissions, and he took a share, as the friend of the two founders, Sir Thomas White and Sir Thomas Pope, in the establishment of St John's and Trinity Colleges at Oxford, receiving the D.D. from the university in 1556 as a token of gratitude. In other quarters, too, his services received rapid recognition. The queen made him Dean of St Paul's in March 1554, and he received a bunch of benefices. At the end of 1556 he was appointed abbot of the newly restored Westminster Abbey.

We have no means of knowing whether Feckenham's decision to return to the monastic life was wholly spontaneous or whether it was inspired by a suggestion from Pole or the queen. With his position and reputation, he would inevitably be the leader of any group he joined, and it would seem probable that the first suggestion came from without. The decision was a momentous one for him, for it meant renouncing a lucrative and influential post. Wise after the event, we may think that he gave a hostage to fortune, and lost the stake, but in fact he had already mortgaged the future by his active and resolute defence of Catholic orthodoxy and by his share in the trials of leading heretics. The advent of Elizabeth would have been as disastrous for the dean of St Paul's as it was for the abbot of Westminster. Nevertheless, the sincerity of Feckenham need not be questioned. Though little external change of life was demanded of him as abbot, he accepted all the responsibilities and the radical obligations of a monk, and he was aware of the legate's intention that the revived Westminster should provide a life more regular and austere than that of Evesham thirty years before.

Abbot Feckenham continued to be one of the prominent figures of the reign, speaking in parliament and Convocation, preaching at Paul's Cross and in the Abbey at the opening of parliament, disputing with heretics, assisting at the refoundation of other communities, serving on royal commissions. His principal and lasting service to the Abbey was the rebuilding in simple style of the damaged shrine of the Confessor, and the solemn translation thither of the body of the saint from the place of security in which it had been hidden when the rich shrine was plundered. He received a few jewels from the queen but he was not granted time in which to see to its ornamentation. For this reason, and perhaps also because it was the tomb of a king as well as of a saint, the shrine was unmolested in the next reign and still remains to be a place of pilgrimage in October.

We know nothing of the forebodings of the abbot and his monks when it became clear that the days of Mary and Pole were numbered. The queen was duly buried at Westminster, and the abbot preached from a text which may have borne heavy undertones for the preacher: 'Wherefore I praised the dead which are already dead more than the living which are yet alive. Yea, better is he than both which hath not yet been.' A month later Elizabeth was crowned in the Abbey, and Feckenham and his monks were there, though their ceremonious movements were not, as will be seen, appreciated. It may have been on the occasion of the visit which by old custom the abbot of Westminster paid to the sovereign in connection with the coronation service that Elizabeth expressed her gratitude to Feckenham and made him, as firm tradition asserted, the offer of the primatial see. Shortly after the coronation the queen came to the Abbey for the opening of parliament, and the Mantuan ambassador relates the sequel. 'On arriving at Westminster Abbey the abbot, robed pontifically, with all his monks in procession, each of them having a lighted torch in his hand, received her as usual, giving her first of all incense and holy water; and when her Majesty saw the monks who accompanied her with torches, she said: "Away with those torches, for we see very well." Thereupon Dr Cox, a married priest, preached a sermon in which, after saying many things freely against the monks, he proved by his arguments that they ought to be persecuted and punished by her Majesty.' Feckenham must have seen well enough the way the wind was blowing, even apart from these inauspicious incidents, but he did not allow his forebodings to influence his actions. For almost three months he was in his place in the House of Lords, using his talents in defence of his beliefs. He voted against the Act of Supremacy. He spoke against the Act of Uniformity and the bill dissolving the refounded monasteries. This was clearly the end, and by the last week in May it was reported that most of the monks had doffed their habits. Early in June Feckenham received an offer from the queen that if he would take the Oath of Supremacy and promise to conform in the Abbey to the new order of services he and his monks might stay. He had no hesitation in refusing and when 29 June, the last day for taking the oath, had passed he prepared, in the words of a contemporary, 'to go about his business'. The abbey as a legal entity ceased to exist on 10 July; the late abbot remained in or about the place for almost a year, arranging the transference of property; at last on 22 May 1560, Feckenham was taken to the Tower 'at about viii o'clock of the evening'.

On that evening began what may be called the fourth act of his adult life. During the twenty-four years that remained to him he was in prison or under house arrest save for a few relatively brief intervals. The government, had it so wished, could in due course have driven him into a position where he must either have recanted or died, but for some reason this extreme step was never taken. It was not in general the policy to go to extremes with those who had been priests or monks before the troubles began, and Feckenham, like other *ci-devant* Catholics, had little direct communication, outside prison, with the seminary priests or the Jesuits. He spent several years in the Tower, along with some of the Marian prelates who had refused to conform, and with his customary amiability helped the new dean of Westminster, Gabriel Goodman, to straighten out his accounts and get a grasp of the administration. He took part again in the sharp and useless controversies that were such a feature of the intellectual life of the times; he was quartered on Anglican bishops at Waltham Abbey and Ely and tired them out with his wealth of argument. Andrew Perne, the well-known Cambridge weathercock, later Master of Peterhouse, also took a hand at disputing with him. For a time he was allowed to live on parole in Holborn and later, when his health gave serious trouble, he was even allowed to spend some time at Bath, taking the waters. Finally, he was sent to Wisbech castle, where a kind of concentration camp of priests was about to be established, and where, after his death, the bitter controversy broke out that was to have such tragic consequences for the Catholic cause in England. In consequence, Feckenham spent the last years of his long life at the margin of the tides where in his day fenland and salt-marsh met, in the bishop's castle lapped by water and mists in winter, searched by the east wind in spring, and touched with colour by dandelion and snapdragon in the summer. He was never idle, and when not engaged in controversy wrote tracts and commentaries on Scripture, or put together for those too poor to pay an apothecary the book of remedies that he had picked up long ago from aunts and country cousins. He resisted all attempts to force or to trap him into accepting the Elizabethan religious programme, and to the last answered his opponents good-temperedly but without withdrawing from what he had learned in his youth to be the faith of Catholics. He was never wholly at a loss for funds. Either by saving or investing surplus moneys in the days of preferment, or by salving something from Westminster, or from family legacies in later life, he was comfortably off, and his estate, while he was in prison, was administered by a friend or a relative. He was even able, at every period of his life, to spend money on the poor. It may be that he felt it a duty as a monk to give away all his superfluity in this way. At West-minster he set up a distribution of alms that lasted long after his day. When at Holborn he gave the milk of twelve cows to the sick and poor and constructed an aqueduct for the people, besides providing prizes for the athletes of the locality. When at Bath he built a hospice for the poor, and even at Wisbech he gave money for a causeway and a market cross. Curious as they may seem, these benefactions seem to be for the most part authentic, and Fuller, sixty years later, had heard the tradition of his largesse, 'so that flies flock not thicker about spilt honey than the beggars constantly crowded round him'. He was able to keep two relatives at the university and to leave substantial legacies to those who had been good to him. He died at last, probably towards the end of 1584, and tradition relates that he was enabled to receive Viaticum devoutly shortly before his death. The last abbot of Westminster lies somewhere in Wisbech churchyard.

As will have been seen, we have a very considerable knowledge of the background and events of Feckenham's life; it is evident that from his early days at Oxford till the end of his life he was one with whom contemporaries had to reckon, and to whom they deferred in the daily affairs of life. He rose naturally, despite mischances, to a position of eminence and authority which he did not abuse, and had the lines fallen for him in an age when a man's career could go smoothly forward, there can be little doubt that he would have reached a commanding position in the Church. In the qualities looked for in an archbishop or a secretary of state in times of peace he would have been surpassed by only a few of those who did in fact reach eminence between 1540 and 1580. At the same time he remains, as do so many of his fellows, something of a dim figure. We have samples of his sermons and works of controversy, but no intimate letters or autobiographical details, and no indications whatever of his emotions, his apprehensions, or his personal religion. His long adult life covers almost exactly the generation of ceaseless controversy, when Englishmen were engaged in bitter theological strife of a kind unfamiliar to the modern world and conducted with improvised weapons in an ill-lit and ever-changing scene. The generation before Feckenham, that of Fisher, Erasmus and More, had grown to maturity in a relatively stable world, and met the religious storm with the outlook of the traditional theologian or the tolerant humanist. The generation after him, that of Campion and Whitgift and Hooker, knew that the religious divisions were permanent and used new weapons and a new technique. To Feckenham and his contemporaries the issues were still confused, the result was still uncertain and the theological platforms not yet sharply and irrevocably defined; the disputants, in England at least, are neither integral Tridentines nor fully Protestant or Calvinist; they are indeed not wholly clear in their own minds where they stand, or whither the world is moving; it is only as time goes on that they harden, and even then they have the illusion that intellectual agreement can be reached by debate.

Feckenham, whose formative years at Oxford had been spent in the twilight of scholastic theology and Erasmian piety, had followed the world in the matters of the royal supremacy and the dissolution of the monasteries and had, without apparent repugnance, taken up with a normal clerical career. There was in him, however, no vestige of continental Protestantism, and even while Henry was still alive he was deploring the advances of heresy. His imprisonment and the acrid theological and liturgical disputes of the time seem to have convinced him, as they convinced Gardiner and many other 'Henricians', that a Church tied to the monarch and severed from Rome could not long escape error and chaos. From 1553 onwards Feckenham was consistent in all his actions, maintaining and defending what he considered to be Catholic truth. He was, however, a controversialist rather than a theologian, but of an accommodating temper rare in that age. His mind moved in terms of practical concessions and adjustments; he had neither Pole's forward-looking zeal for reform, nor the unworldly, single-minded missionary devotion of a Campion; he appears sometimes to continue an argument or to suspend decision when a Jesuit or a seminarian would have broken sharply off. Seen in the whole picture of his life, however, and as a man of his generation, he appears an admirable and sympathetic figure if not wholly an heroic one. As a young man he and his friends had felt no call to follow More and the Carthusians; twenty-five years later the choice was clear, but even then Feckenham had no thought of exile; he remained to endure a long and wearing period of imprisonment, never a martyr, but certainly a confessor of the faith.

There is more than one personal description of him. A tradition records that 'he was of mean Stature, somewhat fat, round fac'd, beautiful, and of a pleasant aspect, affable and lovely in Conversation'. A well-informed contemporary saw in him a 'man of an extremely kindly nature, sanguine temperament and thoughtful cast of mind', and we may picture him, in the portrait of which Augustine Baker had heard, 'with a cornered cappe on his head, and some furre appearinge at the end of his cassock sleeve at his wrist'. His good temper in controversy, his merciful demeanour in his days of power, his generosity to the poor and his long durance for conscience' sake have won the praises of bibliographers, antiquaries and historians of Catholic recusants. There is no reason to believe that he would ever have made a great reformer or a deeply spiritual father of his monks, but he is at least a worthy and dignified figure to end a long line of medieval abbots. An eighteenth-century antiquary, repeating an older tradition, records the familiar anecdote, that when Queen Elizabeth wished to speak with him, 'the first Messenger sent to him found him planting Elms, which are still growing in the Garden at Westminster Abbey; nor would he go with the Messenger till he had finish'd the Work he was about'. Whatever the truth of the story, it is fitting that the last old English abbot, the man of Worcestershire, should be associated in the Abbey precinct two centuries later with the tree that in its gracious and majestic dignity veils and beautifies so many Midland villages and lanes.

POSTSCRIPT

WITH the death in captivity of the abbot of Marian Westminster the series of our portraits ends. English monasticism
did not indeed end, but the revival when it came was for more
than two centuries a hidden, exiled thing and in this country,
at least, Feckenham was the last of a long line reaching back
a thousand years to the coming of Augustine to Canterbury.

In a gallery of portraits we are not concerned with the
history of institutions, but we may be allowed to note what
different types of men could be nurtured on the Rule—the
simple, studious monk of Jarrow, Lanfranc the statesman,
Ailred the sensitive abbot and friend, Samson the feudal
prelate, Thomas de la Mare the great magnate, William
More the country gentleman, Feckenham the Tudor divine.
We may think that we see in all of them a common quality,
a humanity of outlook and a lack of all that is rigid and
doctrinaire and unpractical. They are certainly of another
temper to that of the three friars who occur in their midst.
In any case, they show us how an institution and an ideal is
modified as it passes through the centuries, and takes its
colour from its surroundings. In such a gradual transforma-
tion, the crisis comes when the ideal has lost its force and the
surrounding world has imposed its spirit as well as its pattern.
When this happens life may seem to be extinct, as monastic
life seemed to be extinct in Elizabethan England. Ideas and
ideals, however, may be deathless, and the monastic life is a
living force in the modern world. It may well have a part,
if only a limited part, to play in the life not only of the
Western nations but of peoples outside Europe and America
who have a civilization to retain and to renew in a changing
world.

INDEX

Bold figures indicate a main entry.